THE LIFE OF JAMES IV

After a painting by D. Mytens.

James IV.

THE
LIFE OF JAMES IV

BY

I. A. TAYLOR

AUTHOR OF
"QUEEN HENRIETTA MARIA," "QUEEN HORTENSE AND
HER FRIENDS," "MADAME ROLAND," ETC.

WITH AN INTRODUCTION

BY

SIR GEORGE DOUGLAS, Bart.

ILLUSTRATED WITH 17 PLATES,
INCLUDING A PHOTOGRAVURE
FRONTISPIECE, AND A MAP

LONDON
HUTCHINSON & CO.
PATERNOSTER ROW
1913

CONTENTS

CHAPTER I

1473—1479

CHAPTER II

1479—1482

CHAPTER III

1482—1488

v

CHAPTER IV

1488

CHAPTER V

1488—1495

CHAPTER VI

1495

CHAPTER VII

1491—1496

CONTENTS

CHAPTER XII

1503—1508

CHAPTER XIII

1508

CHAPTER XIV

1509—1512

CHAPTER XV

1513

CHAPTER XVI

1513

CHAPTER XVII

1513

CHAPTER XVIII

1513

CHAPTER XIX

1513

CHAPTER XX

1513

APPENDIX

ILLUSTRATIONS

xi

MAP

INTRODUCTION

IF the reign of Alexander the Third be the Golden Age of Scottish History, then perhaps that of James the Fourth may be called the Silver Age—a second period, two hundred years later than the first, when the land had rest from war, and the arts of peace flourished. To James the Third, an unacknowledged child of the Renaissance, it must certainly be counted for credit that he prepared the way for the brilliancy of his successor's court. But if James the Third reveals himself, in face of conditions the most bitterly untoward, as a man of original mind, enamoured of culture, none the less does he betray at every turn his effeminacy and impotence to rule. As Miss Taylor here points out, King James the Fourth had the wisdom to avoid one of the worst dangers that beset the Stewart dynasty : he abstained from making favourites—such as had caused the downfall of his father, and were again, in the persons of Oliver Sinclair, of Rizzio, and of

Bothwell, to prove fatal to his son and to his granddaughter.

But it was, of course, to no such merely negative cause as this that he owed that immense popularity with his subjects, that love alike of noble and simple, which wrapped him round as with a truly royal robe. For it is scarcely too much to say that he shone in every kingly virtue and quality. High personal courage, perfect graciousness, a fine intelligence, associated with breadth of view and a due sense of the responsibilities of his office : these were perhaps his most striking characteristics. Had they at all times worked together in perfect harmony, and in due subordination one to the other, his claim to be one of the very best kings the world had seen would have been incontestable. As it was, he succeeded in raising Scotland to a position of influence among the nations, of which she had so far scarcely dreamed.

But there were times when defects inherent in his very qualities asserted themselves. A king from striplinghood, he had accustomed himself to stand alone, relying solely on his own judgment ; yet there were moments when a cloud obscured that judgment, based as it was on a high spirit, inclining to self-will. For, with all his truly noble qualities, amid all the

brilliancy of his surroundings, there rested upon
James a blight or taint of hereditary hypo-
chondriasis. This is apparent in the violent
fluctuations of his spirits between sensuous
indulgence and religious asceticism, between
energetic action and a phantom remorse ; just
as, in his successor, it was to become apparent
in the moral breakdown of the dark days
succeeding Solway Moss. It reaches its climax
in the last scenes of all, at Flodden field and on
the days preceding the battle. And truly, had
a dramatic poet sought a foil or contrast to the
mingled brilliancy and nobility of James's life,
he could not possibly have found one more
effective than was furnished by the sequel.
What is bitterest in the tragedy is that it was
all so utterly uncalled-for, unnecessary, wantonly
provoked ! One could scarce have wondered,
indeed, if an age so abundantly superstitious
had come to regard the catastrophe as the work
of some dæmonic agency blindly working out a
doom.

The causes of the war were for the most part
so wholly inadequate—the Queen of France's
gage, the Queen of Scotland's legacy from her
brother or her father. And, again, the psy-
chology of the King's motives is so obscure—
excepting only his firm determination to repel

all guidance, to resist all interference with his
fate. Viewed in this half-fanciful light, the
veteran Surrey readily assumes the character of
destiny incarnate—a fateful figure who twice
already had crossed James's path at critical
points in his career: first, to receive and
refuse his challenge to single combat in the
campaign of 1497; and, secondly, to bring
home his English child-wife. Their third meeting was to prove crucial; nor is one surprised
to read that, according to one historian, James
fell " not a lance's length from where Surrey in
person was fighting." [1] Was this mere chance,
or are we to believe that the old-time antagonists were deliberately seeking one another out
through the on-coming darkness of that autumn
night and of Scotland's waning fortunes?

If we leave at once the imaginative and the
superficial aspect of the war of 1513, it may be
that the true causes of that war must be sought,
not so much in isolated incidents—such as the
murder of the Warden Kerr or the defeat of
Andrew Barton—as in the character and circumstances of the nations involved. Let us
not forget that the peace of 1503, designed
though it was to last for ever, was the first
peace (not truce) the rival nations had known

[1] *Infra*, p. 289.

for one hundred and seventy years. War between them was, then, a habit too deeply ingrained and of too long standing to be broken off all at once; whilst the incident before Norham Castle in the year 1498 serves to illustrate the provocative temper of the neighbours even in time of truce.

Again, it has been suggested that there may have existed in James's mind, when he mustered his forces and crossed the Border, the statesmanlike design to anticipate, or prevent, that disturbance of the existing balance of power which must follow on Henry's possible success in his French campaign. And between their old enemy and their old ally, as James well knew, his people would not hesitate for a moment. But, so far as I am aware, no documentary evidence of any such purpose on the King's part has been brought forward. It remains conjectural, whilst proof abounds that the minor causes of war were actively irritant. Trifles and great issues, fact and fiction, theory and surmise, are indeed most perplexingly clustered about Flodden, and Miss Taylor has certainly done well to tell her readers, with due differentiation, not only what has been ascertained as fact, but also what has been taken for such. For few of the Flodden traditions are wholly

b

untenable, excepting perhaps that of the survival of the King after his reputed death—a fable which had already entertained the popular imagination in the cases of King Arthur, of Barbarossa, and of Richard the Second.

GEORGE DOUGLAS.

THE LIFE OF JAMES IV

CHAPTER I

1473—1479

Birth of James—Condition of Scotland at the time—His father and his two uncles—James III's character a presage of misfortune—Mar's death and Albany's exile.

ON St. Patrick's Day, March 17th, 1473—or, as some say, a year earlier—James Stewart was born. Destined to become the fourth Scottish King of his name, his premature death, forty years later, on the mournful field of Flodden, was to add yet another tragic chapter to the history of a line doomed to misfortune.

At the time of his birth comparative peace and prosperity prevailed in Scotland. England was, if not friendly, in no active condition of hostility, and the truce that had been arranged between the two chronic belligerents was renewed when the heir to the Scottish throne was

I

a week old. Burgundy and Scotland had been united in close bonds of unity by the marriage of his grandfather, James II, with Mary of Gueldres ; to whom, on her husband's death, it had fallen to wield the chief power in the State during the earlier years of her son's minority. With Louis XI of France relations had been also amicable. A wrangle of long standing with Denmark had been ended by James III's marriage with Margaret, daughter of King Christian, and the practical cession to Scotland of the Orkney and Shetland Isles.

All was therefore well abroad ; and at home the King's policy, or his lack of policy, with regard to matters domestic, had not had time to take effect and to prove—as it was to prove in the future—the destruction of the peace and well-being bequeathed to the nation by his father. Nor had the great nobles recovered the power and influence they had temporarily lost or become once again a terror to lesser men and a danger to the Crown.

Yet, whilst all was outwardly prospering, a presage of misfortune must have been contained, to observant eyes, in the character and disposition of the representative of royalty. To obtain a true idea of the atmosphere in which the new-born prince, half Scot, half Dane, was to grow up, the nature and habits of his father are important factors to be taken into account, leading up, as they appear almost inevitably to have done, to the catastrophe which was to make the boy King at fifteen and was likewise to cast so deep and lasting a shadow over his future life.

Of the three sons borne by Mary of Gueldres to her husband, the eldest was, unhappily, the man most incapable of filling his position with honour and success. The second brother, Alexander, Duke of Albany, five years younger than James, was a brilliant figure, of noble presence and knightly gifts, well qualified, at least externally, to appeal to the imagination of the common people, to maintain the royal dignity and to check the spirit of insubordination always ready to show itself amongst the upper classes. Though himself full, as the sequel was to make plain, of soaring ambition, and ill content to play the part of a subject, he might have proved a protection to James against the disloyalty of others, being "so doubted [redoubted] amongst the nobility of the realm that they durst never rebel against his brother the King so long as they were at one."

They were not destined to continue at one. Suspicion and distrust on the one side, a scheming brain and restless aspirations on the other, were quickly to dissolve a union in which both might have found strength and safety. Albany was to end his days in foreign exile, James to fall a victim to his revolted nobles.

The third brother, the young Earl of Mar, six years the King's junior, was so early removed by death from the scene that the praise or blame awarded him by differing authorities must stand chiefly as representing their own conjectures and leanings. The most that can be said with certainty is that he was a tall, handsome lad, fond of sport, a zealous horse-breeder, "comely in all his behaviour," according to one chronicle, "and knowing nothing but nobility."

Such being the estimation in which James's brothers were held, the contrast presented by the King was the more marked; nor was it likely to be overlooked by a nation in no wise blindly devoted to the sovereign power. Already, during his son's childhood, those elements were at work which were destined to render the latter part of James III's reign

" a theatre spread over with mourning and stained with blood." [1] Though outward tranquillity might be preserved, the nation was disunited at home, and so hated abroad that, according to the account of the Sub-prior of Santa Cruz, the mere mention of the name of Scotland was sufficient to rouse men to passion. Its traditional enemy, England, was in particular, in spite of the truce, ever on the alert to make capital out of her neighbour's misfortunes and crimes; to fan ill-feeling between the rival factions in the State; to excite disloyalty towards the Crown, and to turn that disloyalty to her own advantage.

At home, the nobles, at enmity with each other, if forced to keep the peace, would remain sullenly quiescent, maintaining a close watch upon their foes, like animals prepared to spring as soon as an opportunity should offer, when suddenly the smouldering animosity would find vent in defiance of any species of law or authority. At one time it would be the Hepburns and the Homes who were dominant; at another, the Boyd clan would have gained the mastery; the sovereign, standing between them, liable to be caught in the meshes of

[1] Drummond.

the one party or the other, each eager to compass their objects and to effect the ruin of their adversaries, and striving to make use of the royal authority as a means to further their private and personal ends.

It was manifest that, so long as this temper of mind prevailed in the country, peace could be only precariously maintained. Were the central authority to be vindicated and the vessel of State kept from driving upon the rocks, the hand of the pilot must have been steady and strong. Since James III had been of an age to act for himself the man at the helm had been neither strong nor wise, and the natural consequences were to ensue.

Nevertheless, however weak and incompetent as a ruler, James has met with scanty justice at the hands either of his contemporaries or of some, at least, amongst later historians, who have had little but condemnation to bestow upon a sovereign rather the victim of circumstances and of his nature than altogether responsible for the ruin that overtook him.

In certain respects, indeed, he suffered from being in advance of his age. At a day when war was the main occupation and the delight of the majority of men, and their reputation was measured, like that of some Indian tribes, by the number of scalps won from their enemies, James hated fighting, and preferred to the profession of a soldier the practice of arts in the eyes of the fierce and rugged nobles who stood around the throne effeminate and unworthy of the attention of a King or a man. He was fond of architecture, many of the noted buildings of Scotland dating from his reign; was interested in the decoration of churches and gardens, was a lover of letters, and, above all, of music—a taste inherited by his son. Amongst the rude and turbulent men to whom he was an object of contempt rather than of loyal veneration, he was in some sort a stranger and a foreigner in his own country, cut off from his natural associates not only by the admixture of alien blood, which, shared with most sovereigns, places them at a disadvantage compared with their pure-bred subjects, but by reason of the more fundamental differences of tastes and interests. Had he taken his place from the first as King, and thrown himself into affairs of State, public spirit might have supplied a common standing-ground; but, having been deliberately and intentionally encouraged to neglect the study of matters of business during

his minority by counsellors who desired to
retain the management of public affairs, he had
never acquired the habit of giving his attention to such questions. Again, in contrast with
the lavish and ostentatious liberality prac-
tised by his brothers, his frugality and economy
caused him to be accused of an undue love of
money. More unfortunate than all was his
choice of companions. With a natural shrink-
ing from the society of the rough soldiers with
whom he had little in common and of whose
contempt he was probably uneasily conscious,
estranged, as time went on, from those connected with him by the ties of kinship, he
selected as his associates men, to whatever
class they might belong, in whom he found, or
thought he found, kindred spirits. Cochrane,
his favourite in chief, was by profession an
architect, or, as he was called in scorn, a
mason. Another was one Rogers, an English
musician of repute. Ireland, a scholar entertained at court, had been educated abroad; and
to these men were added others of lower birth,
such as Homyl, the royal tailor, fencing-
masters, and the like. To make access to
the King difficult or impossible, whilst he
spent his days surrounded by these parasites,

IACOBVS . III . REX . SCOTORVM .

JAMES III, KING OF SCOTLAND.
From an old print.

was not a mode of attaching the nobles to his person or of inspiring loyalty or affection ; and the time was to come when James would be made to pay heavily for the indulgence of his preferences.

Through the years of his little son's childhood the breach was constantly widening between the men who should have stood nearest to the throne and their master. More and more James fell under the domination of the favourites, whose interest and safety lay in completing the alienation of his natural associates. In a special weakness of the King's, destined to prove disastrous in no common degree, they were to find a powerful auxiliary. The fact that he was steeped in the superstition common at the day was well known to those who had no scruple in turning it to their advantage. Even his rejoicing at the birth of his heir is said to have been clouded by misgivings due to the position of the planets, and the distrust of the infant thus originated was to increase and bear bitter fruit in after years.

For the present, however, the boy was a valuable asset in the hands of his father, and could be made of use in securing the continu-

ance of peace with a troublesome and dangerous
neighbour. At two years old the child was
solemnly betrothed to Cecilia, youngest daughter of Edward IV, a year or two older than her
affianced husband, on terms eminently satisfactory to his father. The truce at present in
force, to last to 1519, was ratified and confirmed; the bride was to bring a dowry of
20,000 marks, to be paid by instalments beginning at once, and the marriage was to take
place as soon as the children should have
reached the necessary age.

So far all had gone well, and James III,
young as he still was, might have looked on
with hope and confidence to the future. But
the elements of disaster were busily at work.
Already his mind was being poisoned by the
men who played at will upon his superstitious
terrors. Prophecies were discovered or invented calculated to serve their purpose. A
Scottish lion was to be devoured by his whelps,
and warnings that danger was to be apprehended from his closest of kin roused in him
mistrust first of his brothers and next of his
son. Whether or not he deliberately avoided
his heir, all pleasure in him must have been
destroyed, and the boy seems to have been

left to the care of his mother, "as wise as she was fair."

To the nobles a monarch of this nature could not be other than an object of anger and aversion. To men, however loyal, who cared for the royal dignity and reverenced the Crown, his conduct was a cause of bitterness and grief. From one of these, at least, he heard the truth; when Patrick Graham, Archbishop of St. Andrews, wrote from his prison at Dunfermline a remonstrance couched in no courtier-like language. As the ecclesiastic of most mark in the country, Graham had been named by the Pope Primate of Ireland and papal legate, and through his reforms had incurred the hatred of traffickers in church preferments and of the clergy into whose lives and morals he had been directed by Rome to inquire. The struggle had been brief and the Archbishop had been worsted in it. William Scheves, chief of his enemies, who had studied astrology at Louvain and combined with his ecclesiastical duties the post of physician and astrologer to the King, was appointed to the see of St. Andrews in his stead, and Graham lay in prison—"a man desolate and forgotten," says Drummond, "as if there had not been such a man in the world."

The King, however, was to be reminded of his existence, and from his place of captivity the Archbishop sent him a letter of rebuke and warning. To seek to gain knowledge by the stars, was, he told him, great ignorance, and oracles left a man in a wilderness of folly. There was no other difference between necromancy and astrology save that in the one men ran voluntarily to the devil, and in the other ignorantly.

It was plain speaking, but useless. Others than the captive Archbishop possessed the King's ear, and events were hurrying on. Albany, as Governor of Berwick and Warden of the Marches, had fallen out with the Hepburns and the Homes, and, though they were no match for him in fair fight, they were bent upon his ruin. Cochrane, chief in favour at court, was easily induced to lend his aid ; and again the King's superstitious terrors were counted upon as valuable auxiliaries in enabling the conspirators to carry out their purpose. It was true that James had loved his brothers, but fear could be trusted to cast out love, and its assistance was to be invoked. A witch was pressed into the service of the Princes' enemies ; and, brought into the royal presence, once more warned the King that he was destined to be slain by his nearest of blood. The revelation, she added, had been made to her by a familiar spirit, and though James appeared at first sight to resent the imputation contained in the prophecy, the poison worked. The Homes and Hepburns, called into counsel, gave it as their opinion that the prediction was true ; and Cochrane, probably well paid for his co-operation, diligently fostered his master's growing distrust and suspicion.

It was unfortunate that at the moment the conduct of Albany and Mar was such as to give colour to the insinuations of those bent upon their destruction. Young and rash, and indignant at the state of the court, Mar is said to have " begun the Tragedy," by reproaching his brother to his face for his familiarity with the contemptible persons by whom he was surrounded, and railing at the misgovernment of the State, till, in a fit of passionate resentment, the King ordered the boy out of his presence. Albany, for his part, had broken on the Border the truce with England, had used his official power to attack his private enemies, and had gathered together a band of lawless followers who obeyed his orders without fear or scruple.

Under these circumstances the King may

have justifiably felt that he had cause for anger; whilst the fears inspired by the soothsayers rendered him the more prompt to use any pretext for placing both brothers where they could do no harm.

Recent events had made it additionally clear that either the King's favourites or his brothers must fall. It was known that a meeting had been summoned by the Princes at which the means to be taken in order to clear the court of the men by whom it was infested had been under discussion—a proceeding amounting to a declaration of war.

Young Mar was the first to feel the weight of James's wrath. To his other offences had been added a rumour charging him with an attempt to compass the King's death by means of witchcraft, and a waxen image of James was said to be wasting before a fire. What followed has been variously narrated. It is certain that Mar was placed in confinement and that there he died, nor are chroniclers wanting who accuse James of his brother's murder — a charge which clung to him to the end of his life. Another and more credible account of the matter relates that the lad, kept captive in Craigmillar Castle, contracted, in his anger and impatience, a fever ; that, his sickness increasing, the King removed the patient to the Canongate and sent his own physician to attend upon him ; that, after the fashion of the day, his delirium was treated by the opening of a vein, and, too much blood having been let, he fainted and died " unawares," his friends around him. Such is the report made by Drummond, on the authority of an anonymous contemporary, believed to be Bishop Elphinstone, nor is it unlikely to be true. But, given the circumstances, the King's timid and suspicious temper and the prophecy known to have been current with regard to the danger to be apprehended from his next of kin, the darker version of the story would easily find credence and James be charged with having taken the opportunity of removing one of his sources of peril. It was probably in the endeavour to lessen the sympathy felt for the supposed victim that twelve old women were brought to trial and burnt on the charge of having conspired with the young Earl against his brother.

Albany was more fortunate. He too was seized and imprisoned in Edinburgh Castle ; but, inviting his custodians to supper on a certain evening, he drank with them till midnight ;

when, leaving his guests heavy with sleep and wine, he let himself down from the window with the help of his body-servant, and contrived to make his way to the shore, carrying with him his man, whose thigh had been broken in the fall. That he would not leave him behind is one item to be put down to the credit of a man of not too blameless a record. Escaping by ship to Dunbar, he fled thence to France and there dwelt for the present in safety. With the memory of the accident which had befallen young Mar in his mind, he may excusably have considered it well to remain at a distance.

At the time that these events took place the heir to the Scottish throne was seven years old, and the heritage of his father's mistrust was descending to the boy. Mar had gone his way to a place from whence he could be trusted to leave his brother unmolested; Albany had taken refuge in flight. But the little Duke of Rothesay was living and in Scotland; and the persistent predictions of astrologers, witches, and fortune-tellers sounded in his father's ears.

CHAPTER II

1479—1482

James III and his favourites—An English invasion threatened—Scotland in arms—Murder of the King's friends.

ALBANY was a fugitive, transformed from a brother and a natural ally and support into an enemy. Mar was in his grave. James, standing by his own deed solitary, and stained in the eyes of his people with the guilt of fratricide, was left to make head against his enemies and to face the disaffected and turbulent nobles by whom he was surrounded with no better assistance than could be rendered by the low-born flatterers filling his court.

He had not learnt wisdom. He loved the men who were scorned by the nation at large; most of all he loved Cochrane, nor had he learnt to dissemble his love. Rather, by creating him Earl of Mar in his dead brother's place, did he proclaim it in a fashion offensive not only to those watching him with malevolent eyes but to all attached to the royal house.

It was the ex-architect who reigned supreme at court, who was most hated and feared, and whose vengeance overtook every man who attempted to resist his power. Occupying the traditional position of a favourite, he stood between James and his subjects, allowing none to approach the King save men belonging to his faction. Those of the nobles who desired to remain loyal to their sovereign could obtain no place near his person or in his service ; nor could the lords of the council, temporal or spiritual, compete in power and influence with the man by whom he was ruled.

That this condition of things could not last was manifest. To yield obedience to the King was to submit to the authority of the favourite in whose hands he was a tool and a puppet. Met together to discuss the state of the kingdom and the remedies called for by its condition, the great nobles made choice of " a wise man " as their messenger, and sent him to acquaint James with the result of their deliberations. If he would free himself from the domination of ungodly flatterers, and take counsel with his nobles as to the government of the realm, the administration of justice, and the defence of the country from its enemies, then his nobles declared themselves, in the language of the day, ready to live and die with him. On the other hand, should he persist in his present course, they took God to witness that they were innocent of whatever mischief might befall.

Such was the ultimatum brought by the wise man. It was perhaps hardly to be expected that James—he was, after all, in spite of his weaknesses, a King and a Stewart—would consent to grant the demands of the malcontents, enforced by their covert threat. A lonely man, oppressed by fears and possibly burdened by the weight of remorse, his sole comfort lay in the presence of the servants who owed everything to him and in whose affection he believed. To throw them to the wolves, even could he have brought himself to forgo their society, may justly have seemed an unmanly surrender. His answer was an uncompromising refusal to listen to the advice forced upon him. He would put no man out of his company for their pleasure—so he told the nobles—nor, were they all agreed in one voice, would he give ear to their counsel.

For once, though in a bad cause, he had spoken like a King. It would nevertheless have been

better for himself, and better for the men he
refused to abandon, had he adopted the policy
of compliance. As it was, another opportunity
for effecting a reconciliation was lost; and the
nobles bided their time. No soothsayer was
needed to predict that trouble was to come.

Meantime, foreign hostility may have in part
distracted public attention from domestic dissension. The truce with England was practically at an end. Fighting on the Border went
on constantly, success lying now with the
English, now with the Scots. If the royal betrothal was still nominally in existence, the
instalments of the bride's dowry were irregularly
paid; and Edward had manifestly lost all
desire to conciliate his northern neighbours.
Louis XI, uneasy at the amity existing between
the English King and Maximilian of Austria,
was doing his best to stir up strife between
England and Scotland, thus to give Edward an
enemy on his hands at home; and Edward was
ready, as ever, to turn the disaffection prevailing in Scotland to his own account. In 1480
hostilities had begun on the Border, and the
Earl of Angus had attacked Bamborough and
burnt it. In the following year Lord Howard
started northwards with a fleet to avenge these

misdoings, and met with a certain amount of success ; Blackness was destroyed by fire, and eight vessels were carried off as prizes. Early in the year 1482 these guerilla hostilities had developed into actual warfare, and James had been about to cross the Border at the head of a considerable force when a papal mandate, to which he yielded obedience, forbade his advance. It was a time, so the Pope's envoy declared, for all Christian princes to turn their arms 'against the Turks. Scarcely, however, had James desisted from his purpose when he was attacked by sea and land by the English, less swayed by papal admonition, and it became clear that a war could not be avoided. An English invasion was threatened, and the Estates assembled at Edinburgh were hot in their indignation against " the robber Edward, calling himself King of England."

It was plainly necessary to lose no time in taking steps to provide for the defence of the kingdom ; and though James was reluctant to raise an army—his favourites, with good cause, fearing the nobles who would command it as much as, if not more than, the foreign foe—it was impossible to await unarmed the coming of the English.   The muster of all available troops was not made too soon. The Duke of Gloucester, at the head of the English forces, was already marching to lay siege to Berwick, and brought with him not only the Douglas, who had been sent into exile, but the King's own brother Albany, who had crossed over from France and thrown in his lot with the English enemy. Though received with cordiality by Louis on his escape from Scotland, and given in marriage Anne de la Tour, daughter of the Comte de Boulogne et d'Auvergne, he had decided that no practical support in the redressing of his wrongs was to be hoped for from France, and had thereupon applied for help to the traditional foes of his country. The terms he obtained from Edward showed that, whatever may have been the case at an earlier date, James's distrust was now fully justified. The title of King of Scotland was bestowed upon the Duke, and it was settled that, in return for the help Edward was to give him towards rendering his titular sovereignty a reality, he was to do homage to the English King. The fact that he had left a wife in France notwithstanding, it was further arranged that, provided he could make himself clear, according to the laws of the Church, of all other women, he should marry his little nephew's affianced bride, the Princess Cecilia.

There was no doubt that the situation was an anxious one for James. To have his brother and Douglas—upon whose head a price had been set—united with England against him was no light matter. Nevertheless, his domestic troubles, drawing to a head, were more serious still. The time was at hand when the gang of courtiers he had gathered about him were to meet their doom.

More causes than one may have contributed to hasten it. The list of crimes laid to their charge might be long, but conditions for which they could not be justly held responsible had also tended to produce a spirit of discontent throughout the country. If debased coinage had been issued by the King at the instigation of his chosen advisers, corn and cattle had also been destroyed in the Border warfare, and to these two factors combined the hunger and dearth prevailing in the kingdom was ascribed, many of the poor dying of starvation. To add to the sufferings of the people, the winter had been a season of unusual severity. Pain and anger are often seen to go hand in hand, and it is possible that the consciousness that the nation would be prepared to support them in an endeavour to overthrow the existing system of government may have helped to arm the nobles against the King. And the patience of the nobles was exhausted.

In the meantime the troops who had been called out for the defence of the country had assembled on the Borough Muir, to the west of Edinburgh, whence they marched, the King in person at their head, to Lauder. However averse James might be to war, he must have acknowledged that the time to avoid it was gone by. With the King marched his enemies and his friends. Even in this time of war, as before in times of peace, he was at no pains to conciliate the men who held his fate in their hands. He opened the campaign upon which so much depended accompanied by the group of courtiers hated by the nation, and they were kept constantly at his side, to the exclusion of those who had a right, by blood and rank, to a place near the person of their King.

Conspicuous amongst the favourites was Cochrane, " the mason," transcending in magnificence and in the luxury of his appointments the greatest amongst the nobles. The canvas of his tent was of silk, and he was attended by a

bodyguard of three hundred armed men, richly
clad. His riding-dress was of black velvet ; he
wore a heavy chain of gold about his neck, and
a hunting-horn, adorned with gold and with a
precious stone called a burial hanging from it,
was slung across his shoulders. This was the man
whom James, himself noted for frugality and
economy carried to a fault, delighted to honour.
Had his folly and blindness been less, it was
probably too late to avert the blow that was to
fall. The lords were at length in a position to
strike, nor were they disposed to allow the opportunity to slip.

The King had been some days at Lauder
when a strong body of men, under the leader-
ship of Angus, Huntley, Lennox, and several
more of their fellow nobles, reached the town.
Assembled in the church one June night—or, as
some say, in the early morning—the chiefs of
the party of malcontents took counsel together.
Addressing the meeting, the Earl of Angus spoke.
He described the nature of the situation with
which they had to deal—the King surrounded
by evil counsellors and by fortune-tellers, one
brother slain, the other sent to be a leader to
the enemy. Danger threatened all alike, since
the destruction of the men of noble birth was

desired by the favourites. Between Englishmen and Scots the contest was for glory and
empire—Edward was of a generous spirit. Yet,
even did he seek the death of the King, who
should be called the more merciful—the man
who slays outright, or he who daily puts to torture him to whom, next to God, love and obedience is due ; who turns him against those of his
own blood, keeps him captive, and does not
permit him to look on the face of his friends ?
As the case stood, victory would procure
neither peace nor glory, and would only give
added license to their enemies to oppress.
"Wherefore," the orator is represented as con-
cluding, "my opinion is that we first break our
domestic yoke."

The suggestion was received with acclama-
tion. The short summer's night was still dark,
but the crowd who filled the church, catching
fire from Angus's words, would have rushed in
a body to the royal pavilion had they not been
restrained by cooler heads, who feared for the
life of James himself.

Of what followed accounts differ in matters
of detail, but the tale told by the several
chroniclers is substantially in accord.[1] By one

[1] Buchanan. Pitscottie.

of these it is reported that the King, awaking
in fear and learning that the lords were
gathered together, despatched Cochrane to inquire into what was going forward—his choice
of a messenger evidencing his ignorance of what
was in contemplation—and that, meeting certain of the leaders on their way to the royal
tent, the favourite was at once taken into
custody. By other authorities it is stated that
he was at the door of the church before the
chiefs of the party had started on their errand,
and that, knocking at it, he was answered by
Douglas of Lochleven, in charge of the gateway.
Who was it, Douglas asked, who knocked so
rudely ?

"It is the Earl of Mar," answered Cochrane,
still unsuspecting what was to come; "which
news pleased well the council, because they
were ready to take him."

"The victim has been beforehand with us,"
said Angus grimly, as he bade Douglas unbar
the door and admit the Earl and as many of
his accomplices as were there.

"Then the Earl of Angus met the Earl of Mar
as he came in at the kirk door and pulled the
golden chain from his neck and said 'a rope
would suit him better.' Sir Robert Douglas,

seeing this, pulled the blowing-horn from him and said to him 'he had been over-long a hunter of mischief.'"

Even then it would seem that the unhappy man had not grasped his peril, but conceived it possible that the nobles were indulging in rough horse-play.

"My lords," he asked, "is it jest or earnest?"

The answer was ready. He should find it for earnest, they told him. He and his accomplices had long enough abused the King. He was now to reap his reward.

His doom was delayed whilst the chiefs proceeded on their way to the King's tent, leaving the principal culprit behind securely guarded. It is said that conditions were offered to James. If he would consent to recall the debased coinage he and his late advisers had put into circulation and would yield up his favourites unconditionally to justice, the lords would follow him against the enemy. It is to the King's credit that he indignantly refused to comply with these demands. He was, however, helpless in the hands of the nobles. The wretched men who were around him were seized and led out to trial, one only, Sir John

Ramsay, a lad of eighteen, being spared at
James's entreaty and in consideration of his
honourable birth and his youth. Amid shouts
of "Hang the villains!" the rest were taken to
execution, James himself being led forth a
prisoner.

A ghastly scene followed. Over the bridge
at Lauder, the lesser victims were hung before
their master's eyes ; after which James was
brought in person to the council by which
Cochrane was to be tried. It was the last
meeting, face to face, of the two—the King
powerless to save the man he loved, the favourite, his hands tied behind him with a
rope, in spite of his demand that at least the
silken cords of his tent should be used for the
purpose, "for he thought shame to be bound
with a hemp tow like a thief."

No petition he could prefer would have been
granted. He was worse than a thief, was the
stern reply, since he was a traitor ; and his
execution followed quickly. Above the companions who had already suffered death, he too
was hanged from the bridge, and the King
was left friendless and alone. So ended the
doings of that night.

To march against the English under the circumstances, the nobles at war with the King, the King at war with the nobles, was recognised as impossible. Neither would trust the other. For the moment the sense of the domestic situation appears to have banished the fear of the foreign invader. The army was disbanded, and the King taken, a virtual prisoner, to be lodged in Edinburgh Castle. The first open struggle between him and his subjects had ended in their victory. In that struggle his son had taken no share. In the one which was to follow he was to play an important part.

CHAPTER III

1482—1488

The King's position—Treaty with England—Relations of
James and his nobles—John Ramsay—The Duke of
Rothesay removed from Stirling Castle by the rebels
—Father and son opposed to one another—Battle of
Sauchieburn—Death of James III.

THERE can have been few sadder or lone-
lier men throughout the length and breadth
of Scotland, after that night's wild work, than
its King. Up to that day he had been surrounded by those who, whatever might be their
intrinsic demerits, however they might be regarded by others, reflected his tastes, his interests, ministered to his needs, and created
around him a congenial atmosphere. In the
affection of men who owed all to him he doubtless, rightly or wrongly, believed. Suddenly
they were swept away. In a single night, under
his very eyes, every one of his chosen associates
—with the exception of the boy Ramsay—had
been barbarously murdered. Their crime, he

31

may well have told himself, was that they loved him. He was left with a solitude around him, none at hand to whom to turn for sympathy save his rough captors. To them, by virtue of his blood, he represented the sovereign to whom their formal allegiance was due, but they had nothing except contempt for the man who had disgraced his high position. For his Danish wife, beautiful and good, there is no proof to show that he felt any affection, and should his thoughts turn towards his son it would be to remember the prophecy which rendered him an object of terror. To his heir was attached the prediction which had already wrought so much ill. "Next of kin," "the lion's whelp" —to whom should the names apply if not to the boy to whom he was almost a stranger?

Concerning this son little information is available during these early years. Some have asserted that he was shut up, secluded from the outer world like a prince in a fairy tale, so that by these means his father might escape the danger that menaced him. If such was indeed the case, James III was to learn that the decrees of destiny are not thus to be evaded. It appears, at all events, that until the death of his mother, when he was in his fifteenth year, the Duke of Rothesay continued to be left in her hands. It has also been said that Margaret Drummond, whom he afterwards loved so well until her premature death, was a member of the Queen's household. This, however, is scarcely more than surmise, and may owe its birth to the romance that was to follow; nor is it until later that the boy comes tragically into the light, under circumstances that justified only too fully the misgivings by which his father's brooding mind had been haunted and darkened. Fate is not mocked, and prophecies are apt to work towards their own fulfilment.

It is not necessary, in a life of James IV, to do more than summarise the events of the years following upon the massacre at Lauder. Enough has been told to indicate what was the condition of the kingdom he was soon to rule and the difficulties with which he would find himself confronted when his enforced obscurity should end and the fierce glare of publicity would beat upon him.

The drastic remedy applied by the nobles to the results of their sovereign's weakness and folly had left him no more than "a King in phantasy and his throne but a picture." His captors carried on the government in his name;

3

a treaty was concluded with England, according to the terms of which Albany, on condition that he returned to his allegiance, was pardoned all past offences and restored to the posts he had forfeited ; Berwick passed finally out of Scottish hands ; the betrothal of Rothesay to the English princess was shortly afterwards cancelled, and the instalments of her dowry paid were honestly returned. Such were the main features of the pacification.

The alliance between Albany and the confederate lords did not prove lasting ; and though a reconciliation with the King followed upon the release of the latter—obtained by the Duke at the urgent instance, it is said, of the neglected Queen—this too was of brief duration. Renewed distrust on James's part, treasonable practices on Albany's, quickly succeeded to amity and continued till the struggle between the brothers was terminated by the ultimate flight of the Duke to France, where, after gaining a high reputation as " the father of chivalry," he shortly died from a wound received at a tournament. Thus ended the life of James's remaining brother.

It was well for Scotland that domestic troubles had afforded England less leisure than usual for intervention in Scottish affairs. Upon Edward's death had followed the brief reign of the usurper, Richard, with whom James continued on friendly terms, affiancing his heir to another English bride, in the person of Richard's niece, Anne, daughter of the Duke of Suffolk. Nor was peace between the two countries interrupted by the fall of Richard and the accession of Henry Tudor. The engagement to Anne ended with the death of her uncle, but a fresh English marriage was projected for Rothsay, destined, like the two former ones, to come to naught. At peace with England, comparative prosperity had thus marked the five years which succeeded the tragedy at Lauder. But the time was approaching when the sceptre was to pass from the hands of a King who had proved incapable of maintaining the royal dignity.

The Queen was by this time dead, her boy motherless. The nobles, whether or not nominally at peace, were, as ever, divided into parties and factions. Those of them who had taken an active share in the removal of the King's favourites, who had humbled their master and used him as a puppet, were well aware that, though policy might cause James to disguise his rancour, he was not a man to forget or to forgive the part they had played, and that, when it was possible to take vengeance, he would not fail to do so. Watchful and alert, they were ever on their guard against a blow, and had justification for their attitude been needed it was not wanting. Inviting, according to the story told by Buchanan, his old foe, Douglas, to Edinburgh Castle, James made overtures to the man to whom he was bound by a common enmity. The leaders of the faction which had incurred the King's wrath were no friends to Douglas, and James pointed out to the Earl the opportunity that now offered of avenging himself by the apprehension of the leaders of the faction opposed to him. But the King had misread the character of the old chieftain. The methods he suggested, the idea of putting his enemies secretly to death, were repugnant to Douglas's sense of honour. Though he was willing to seize the King's foes openly and to bring them to trial, he not only refrained from acting on James's advice, but conveyed a warning of their danger to the menaced men. The sole result of the affair was to render reconciliation more impossible than before. Any lingering sentiment of loyalty on the part of the nobles could hardly be expected to survive their acquaintance with the blow planned by the King ; whilst James was confirmed by the fact that Douglas had sided with his order against him in his rooted distrust of the nobles and his preference for men destitute of any power and influence save what was derived from him.

For the lesson that had been given him had been fruitless ; and not even yet had he learnt to refrain from the conduct which had brought down so terrible a retribution at Lauder. One man had there escaped the fate of his comrades ; and Ramsay, who had then clung to him for protection, and had been spared at his entreaty, at twenty-three occupied the position of his principal adviser and counsellor. Nor would the lad who had seen his companions dragged to their death and had himself only by a hair's-breadth escaped sharing in their doom be inclined to use his influence in the cause of peace. Jealousy therefore, as time went on, again combined with fear—an ever-present fear of what might befall should the King become sufficiently powerful to execute justice—to arm against him a large proportion of the men of rank and position in the realm.

In some cases private interest, or a private grievance, heightened the hostility common to many ; and to a subsidiary cause of this kind was due the formation of the conspiracy that was to prove the beginning of the death-struggle between the King and his antagonists. The revenues of Coldingham Priory, to which the Homes conceived that they had a right, had been bestowed by James upon the Chapel Royal at Stirling—a foundation in which, as his own creation, he took a personal interest—and, supported by their allies, the Hepburns, the clan had determined upon an armed vindication of their claim.

This special quarrel may have done no more than precipitate the inevitable open rupture. No additional incentive to rebellion was necessary, and, as before, James appeared to rush upon his fate.

With almost incredible imprudence, when the state of the country and of public feeling is taken into account, he had presumed upon the adherence of a certain party in the State to make his attitude towards those of the nobles who were stained with blood dangerously clear. When Parliament met in October 1487 the King's temper had been tested by a proposal that all existing grievances and disputes should be considered by the nobles to be cancelled on condition that a full pardon was granted for all past offences, whether treason, rapine, or any other. It was an overture of peace the King would have done well to accept, at the cost of forgoing an uncertain vengeance. His partisans, however, not only rejected it, absolutely and conclusively, but further showed their hand by the introduction of an act which, regretting the delay in inflicting "sharp execution upon traitors and murderers," declared that no remission of crimes of this nature was to be granted for the space of seven years. What was tantamount to a deliberate menace of the lords—and they were many—who could be convicted of treason or of murder had been ventured, and the men at whom it was aimed took their measures accordingly.

At this point James, Duke of Rothesay, at length comes definitely into view. It was a year since he had lost his mother; having learnt, it may be, before her death—for he was not backward in such matters—to understand and resent the neglect shown her by a husband who preferred the society of his favourites, men and women—especially one of these last called the Daisy—to that of his wife. If the assertion that the boy had grown up without so much as knowing his father by sight is hardly credible, the fact that it gained currency is significant of the terms believed to exist between father and son ; nor is it impossible that James, a victim of his superstitious terrors, should have felt a nervous aversion to intercourse with the boy who embodied them.

The time had, however, arrived when the heir to the throne could be no longer ignored. Though little is known of the Prince up to this date, he had reached an age when, in the fifteenth century, childhood had long been left behind. It also seems clear that, in his sixteenth year, he was far in advance of his age. His spirit was bold and adventurous, and the tact, firmness, and judgment marking the early years of his reign were not qualities to have been suddenly developed and must have been maturing in the seclusion of his boyhood. To a nature as many-sided as James's was to show itself, with interests varied and vivid, it must have been specially galling to be sedulously kept in the background and rendered of no account in the country he would one day rule. As he gradually realised his wrongs he may easily have become embittered towards the man who was responsible for them, and have felt himself exonerated from the duties of a son towards a father who had performed none of those corresponding to them. It is true that the remorse, carried to the point of morbidness, which haunted and overshadowed his future life, indicates a singularly sensitive conscience, when the standard of the day and the general indifference towards deeds of violence is taken into account. But in the excitement of the moment when the opportunity of emancipation was offered him, the issues of the struggle upon which he was invited to enter might have become confused, and older men may have found little difficulty in overcoming such scruples as he felt.

To the party in the State opposed to the King it was of the last importance to obtain the countenance of the heir to the throne and by this means to safeguard themselves from the charge of disloyalty to the royal house. This they set themselves accordingly to do; determined to leave no means untried to compass the object they had in view; and, whilst using their best endeavours to conciliate the Prince, they did not hesitate to add the threat that, failing his co-operation in their designs, they would be compelled to turn to England for support.

Whether Rothesay yielded with eagerness or with difficulty to their solicitations there is no certain evidence to show. Some authorities allege that, in the scenes that were to follow, he was a victim, a mere figure-head, rather than a voluntary agent. Their hypothesis does not carry conviction. Had James given way to coercion alone, it is not probable that his penitence for the share he had in his father's downfall would have proved so deep and lasting.

When the crisis arrived he was in the fortified castle of Stirling, where he had been placed by his father in the charge of one Schaw of Sauchie, to whom the King had given strict orders that, as he loved his honour and his life, he would neither permit any person to enter the fortress or allow the young Duke, upon any pretext, to leave it. Whether the injunction was dictated by solicitude for the boy's safety in the disturbed condition of the country or by other motives, the species of captivity to which he was subjected must have gone far to incline a high-spirited boy to lend an ear to the accusations brought against his father and to listen to the overtures of those he would regard as his deliverers.

Meantime, James himself had withdrawn to the north, to rally his forces and to prepare for the imminent trial of strength with those of the nobles who were by this time in open rebellion. That he entertained suspicions of the disposition of his elder son may be inferred from the fact that he had taken steps to bring the younger into prominence, by creating him Duke of Ross and heaping upon him other titles, as if to point to the child as of future importance. For the present, there was every prospect of his being strong enough to hold his own against the insurgent forces. Roughly speaking, it was in the south alone that the conspirators had found confederates, the northern provinces remaining true to their allegiance. In Fife, whither James proceeded with the adherents he had collected in the north, he was met by Lord Lindsay—a leader well versed in the art of war —at the head of a body of men four thousand strong, and riding a great grey charger, from which he dismounted, to present it to the King. Should James need either to fly or to pursue—so he told him—that horse would do his pleasure better than any in Scotland. His master, "thanking him gladly," accepted the gift. Yet there were those who looked upon it as ominous.

It is difficult, reading the confused and conflicting accounts of different historians, to follow with accuracy the sequence of events at this juncture, or to decide at what date James was made aware that his son was no longer in safe keeping, that the rebel nobles had obtained possession of his person, and that it was in their power to declare that it was on his behalf and in his name that they drew their swords against his father. By bribes and promises, Schaw had been wrought upon to place the Prince in their hands, and further to pledge himself to hold Stirling Castle in his name and to refuse admission, if need be, to the King himself.

Nor is there any valid reason, in spite of his apologists, to doubt that Rothesay was found ready for the adventure. Taking for granted a lack of any deterrent affection for his father, it would have been strange if it had not been so. It is easy to imagine the excitement of a boy of fifteen, suddenly released from durance, and marching to Linlithgow at the head of a body of men whose interest it was to flatter him, to

WATCH TOWER AND BATTLEMENTS, STIRLING CASTLE, FROM N.E. CORNER OF THE PALACE.

Photo by Francis C. Inglis.

win his affection and confidence, and who, posing as his champions, painted his father's conduct in the blackest of colours and stimulated both his fear and anger.

At Linlithgow a proclamation was put forth, calling upon all men to flock to the defence of the heir to the crown. The King was declared to be suspicious of his son, as before of his brother, and to be coming with an armed force to take the Prince prisoner. Rothesay probably believed what he was told, and the days went on, adding each its share of material for the remorse destined to haunt him to the grave.

James, meanwhile, ignorant of what had passed at Stirling,[1] is said to have presented himself before the castle, demanding entrance, and, being refused it by the custodian he himself had left in charge, asked to have speech with his son. The reply was at first evasive, but when the King, though still gently, reiterated his demand, and inquired as to the whereabouts of the boy, Schaw admitted part, at least, of the truth. The Prince was gone, taken from him, he protested, against his will.

[1] This is Lindsay of Pitscottie's account. According to some other authorities the visit to Stirling was only paid on the eve of the final struggle, when the King was well aware of his son's escape.

Then the King's anger broke forth. He had been deceived, and he vowed to God that, should he live, he would be avenged upon the traitor and reward him as he deserved.

To the boy he sent messengers, striving to recall him to his duty. Whatever may have been his vague fears, that his heir should take the field openly against him was doubtless a blow. But his overtures were fruitless. Those who had the Duke in their power had gone too far to recede. If there had been no place for repentance for the slayers of Cochrane and his comrades, their case was now doubly desperate. Upon that assumption they acted. The Duke of Rothesay was proclaimed King, and when negotiations were set on foot with England, Henry VII played into their hands by consenting to treat with the Prince as a fellow sovereign. Father and son being pitted against one another and the issue of the struggle uncertain, the first of the Tudors—always cautious—was anxious to prepare for every contingency.

James had also made his appeal to England, and letters from him had been received, asking for help. France and the Pope had likewise been called upon to intervene. What answers were returned by England and France does not appear ; but that some attempt at mediation was made by both is to be inferred from the statement that to each of these Powers the rebel nobles replied that peace could only be obtained on condition that James would abdicate. The legate despatched by Pope Innocent, for his part, arrived, in the language of the chronicler, a day after the fair. When he reached England on his way north he learnt that his intervention would come too late and was advised to go no farther.

The domestic belligerents were thus left to settle their quarrel themselves. The first skirmish — it could hardly be called more — took place at Blackness, when the royal troops were victorious. Again James made overtures of peace. He had no inclination to be unduly severe, and the terms he offered, in his moment of success, were marked by indulgence, if not by weakness. In return for certain concessions —a recognition of the prerogatives of the crown and of the royal authority—a free pardon was promised to all the supporters of the Prince, and he himself was to be left in the hands of his present advisers, " provided they were honourable and faithful persons." The negotiations were carried on between father and son on an equal footing, and a pacification as unlikely to endure as could well be imagined was concluded. After which, with incredible imprudence, James disbanded his army. Scarcely had he done so when the insurgents were again in the field ; his own adherents rallied to the royal banner, and preparations were made for a final trial of strength.

It took place in the neighbourhood of Stirling. Shut out of his royal castle, the question of a siege was under the King's consideration, when news was brought that the rebel forces were encamped upon the high ground above the bridge of the Torwood. In battle array the royal troops marched forward to meet them. Confident in his strength, James was determined to fight, and lent a deaf ear to counsellors who would have had him, at the eleventh hour, treat with the men arrayed against him. Mounted on the great grey horse Lindsay had given him, with Lindsay at his side, he watched the advance of the enemy from the brow of a hill as they moved into sight. The Homes and the Hepburns led the way, followed by the main body of the rebels, the Prince in person—having, it is said, given orders that no

man should lay hands upon his father—acting
as their general, the rebels hastening forward
the more confidently "because they knew . . .
the King was neither hardy nor constant in
battle." Once again James's character, the reputation he bore, was his misfortune.

And how was it in that last hour with
James ? It may be that some of his faithful
followers, who stood there at his side, made
afterwards relation of their master's anguish,
and that from their lips the chronicler heard
the story he tells. The situation indeed justified anguish. Peace-loving, a man destitute
of martial ardour and enthusiasm, he saw
himself forced into a death-struggle with his
subjects, led by his son ; was conscious, it may
be, that by his ineptitude and indolence he had
invited the ruin which might overtake him.
He may have divined that even those who
were around him, staunch and loyal to their
sovereign as they were, despised him as a man.
Below him, his troops were awaiting the enemy's
attack ; the advancing columns of the rebels
were moving into sight under his own royal
banner, his heir at their head. And, as he
watched them, he is said to have called to
mind the witch's prophecy that he was fated

to be suddenly destroyed by his nearest of kin.

That recollection put the last touch to the horror of the scene, and superstition sapped what courage he possessed; the nobles at his side perceiving his alarm and urging him, whether with secret contempt or with a genuine desire to ensure his safety, to "pass by the host till they had fought the battle."

Meantime, the result of the encounter had at first appeared doubtful, the advantage lying alternately with the rebels and with the royalists; but as the fierce borderers—the "thieves of Annandale"—rushed shouting into the fight, the royal forces wavered; the tide of battle was seen to sweep onwards towards the spot where James was stationed; the advice of those who recommended flight, seconded by terror, got the better of his courage, and, turning his horse's head from the field of battle, he struck his spurs into him and galloped towards the town of Stirling. He was not destined to reach it. Alone, unattended, the King of Scotland rode at breakneck speed through the village of Bannockburn. As he crossed the stream which gave it its name, a woman who was carrying water to the mill-house, scared by the furious rider, threw down her pitcher and fled. Startled at the sound, the great grey horse leapt the stream, stopped suddenly short at the mill-house, and the King, no expert horse-man, was thrown violently to the ground, where, weighted with his heavy armour, he swooned away. The grey horse had done his work.

Ignorant of his rank, and only perceiving that a man lay fainting at their door, the miller and his wife carried him in, still unconscious, and laid him on a couch. The sequel has been variously told. It would seem that, coming presently to himself, James begged urgently for a priest to whom he might confess; whereupon the miller and his wife asked what man he was and what was his name.

"He happened to say, unhappily, 'This day at morn I was your King.' Then the miller's wife clapped her hands and ran forth and cried for a priest," publishing abroad for whom his services were required.

A priest, or a man who assumed that charac-ter, named Borthwick, chanced to be passing, and offered his services with alacrity.

"Here am I, a priest," he told the woman. "Where is the King?"

Brought at once to the penitent, whom he knew by sight, he knelt down by him, asking if James did not think he might live if he had good treatment. To which the King answered he thought he might ; he needed a priest, however, to counsel him and give him the Sacrament.

"That shall I do hastily," answered Borthwick, and, taking out a dagger, he struck his victim to the heart, repeating his blows till he was dead.

So died James III, leaving an unquiet heritage to his son, as well as a lifelong remorse.

CHAPTER IV

1488

THE battle was over; the rebels were triumphant; the King lay in the mill-house
dead, or, as some say, had been carried away
by the murderer. Nevertheless, as yet no one
had seen his body or could positively declare
that the kingdom had passed to his son. Either
the man who had slain him was in no haste to
proclaim his achievement, or it may have seemed
difficult to believe that the King of Scotland
should have met his death, not on the field of
battle, but alone, defenceless, and in obscurity,
like any common victim of crime. At all events,
it is clear that for a time a considerable degree of
uncertainty was felt as to his fate. James might
be in hiding, preparing to collect his forces; he
might, more likely, have escaped abroad. The

famous sea-captain, Sir Andrew Wood, of stainless loyalty, was known to be hovering about the coast, with his two great ships, the *Yellow Carvell* and the *Flower*. Many wounded royalists had been taken from the shore to be cared for on board. Was not their master of their number?

Under these circumstances the rebel nobles, with the Prince, proceeded to Linlithgow and thence to Leith, there to await tidings which would place them in a position to take decided steps. From Leith messengers were sent to demand of Wood whether the King was on board his vessels or no. "[Wood] said he was not there, and bade them search and seek his ships at their pleasure, if they believed not him." Still unsatisfied, the lords again despatched messengers, requiring on this occasion that Wood should come to Leith in person, to answer the questions of the Council. Lord Seaton and Lord Fleming having been sent as hostages for his safety—no unnecessary precaution—Sir Andrew obeyed the summons and repaired to Leith, where, according to the chronicler, a singular scene[1] took place : "As soon as the Prince saw the captain himself before him [he]

[1] This is believed by some historians to be incredible.

LINLITHGOW PALACE.

From an old print.

54]

believed surely it had been his father, and inquired of him,

" ' Sir, are you my father ? '

" Who answered, with tears falling from his eyes, ' Sir, I am not your father ; but I was a servant to your father, and shall be to the authority till I die, and an enemy to them that was the occasion of his down-putting ? ' "

Asked by the lords what he knew of the King and where he was, Wood protested his ignorance. Who, then, had it been, he was further demanded, who had come from the battle-field and been removed to the ships ?

" It was I and my brother," he answered boldly, " who were ready to have risked our lives with the King in his defence. He is not in my ships," he added, again pressed for a definite answer, " but would to God he were in my ships safely. I should defend him and keep him skaithless from all the treasonable creatures who have murdered him, for I think to see the day when they shall be hanged and drawn for their demerits."

After which denunciation he took leave, the lords ill content, as they well might be, with his despiteful answers and proud speaking, yet afraid, for the sake of the men who were hostages in his vessels, to lay hands upon him. He was therefore dismissed in haste. Seaton and Fleming returned to Leith, explaining that, had Wood been longer detained, they would not have escaped with their lives.

The hostages in safety, it was considered desirable to lose no time in securing the bold opponent who had so uncompromisingly denounced his master's enemies ; and the skippers of Leith were assembled and offered all needful supplies of men, artillery, and provisions if they would undertake his capture. It was, however, in vain. So great was Sir Andrew's reputation that no bribes could induce the mariners of Leith to go to sea against him. No ten ships in Scotland would give battle to Wood and his two—so one Barton, doubtless a member of a noted family of seamen, declared. Relinquishing, therefore, the hope of reducing the great captain to submission by force of arms, the Prince and his friends repaired to Edinburgh, where the castle surrendered without a struggle. The King's body having been by this time found, it was given royal burial, the treasures he had amassed were seized, arrangements were made for the future government of the country, the offices of State were,

not unwisely, filled, and before the end of June
the new sovereign, James IV, had been
crowned at Scone.

From Scone he proceeded to Stirling, there to
take up his abode for a time ; and here it was
that the dogs of remorse appear to have flung
themselves upon him.   Already before the final
and fatal battle, his conscience had been uneasily stirred by the remonstrances of certain
adherents of the royal cause who had gained
access to him.   But at that moment the excitement of the struggle and the influence of the
men who had steeled his mind against his father
had probably availed to keep his misgivings at
bay.   It was a different matter now that the
fight was over ; what had been done was irre-
parable, and he was at leisure to look the
facts in the face.

Nor was Stirling Castle a place where they
could be readily forgotten.   It had been the
favourite home of the dead King—"he took
such pleasure to dwell there," says Pitscottie,
"that he left all other castles and towns in
Scotland."   To it he had added, perhaps by
Cochrane's advice, the great hall.   He had also
established the religious foundation which
had been a cause of quarrel with the Hepburns

and Homes. Called the Chapel Royal, it had a complete chapter of ecclesiastical dignitaries and a double number of musicians and choristers, so that half of them should be ready at all times to accompany him wherever he might go, " to sing and play with him and hold him merry," their comrades the while attending to their duties at Stirling.

Now, in the place his father had loved, the boy King was overwhelmed with horror at the consciousness that he was in some sort responsible for the doom that had overtaken him, and was guilty of his blood. Throughout James IV's life, in spite of the laxity of morals he shared with many of his contemporaries, religion was ever a powerful element in his character; he was liable to fits of brooding melancholy, alternating with gaiety and high spirits. As at Stirling Castle he listened daily to the mattins and evensong sung by priests and choristers who looked back to the late King as their founder, as he heard the prayers offered for the soul of the murdered man, as mourning and lamentation sounded in his ears, it was no wonder that the conscience of the son who occupied his place should have been troubled. Anxious and ill at ease, oppressed by the burden of his guilt, the lad sought counsel of a priest belonging to the chapel as to how he might be freed from its weight.

His chosen adviser found himself in a difficulty. James was young and could not be trusted to be secret. The men in power—Angus, who filled the post of the King's guardian, at their head—were the very men who had induced him to take part against the dead King; to them was owing the crime he deplored; his guilt, if guilt it were, was in double measure theirs; to endorse his self-condemnation would be to condemn those with whom he was associated. Such being the case, and the ecclesiastic to whom he had applied being in no wise desirous of drawing down vengeance on his own head, he thought it well to use economy of truth and not to speak all that was in his mind. What he dared do he did. "Thinking they would be utterly displeased at him if he had desired the King to do that which became him"—it is not specified what that was — "he comforted the King in the time of his repentance, and continued his counsel until his Grace was further stricken in age."

The boy, with his keen intelligence, is not

unlikely to have divined the motives of his timorous adviser. Notwithstanding the consolation thus prudently administered, he remained "sad and dolorous," and selecting a self-inflicted penance, caused an iron belt to be made which he wore round his waist until the day of his death, adding additional links to its weight every third year.

The King's melancholy and the King's remorse were both calculated to supply subject-matter for reflection and misgivings to the men who had caused them; and they did their best to dispel them. Amusements were devised to distract his mind from thoughts of the past—dancing, plays, hunting-parties, filled his days; whilst it is also stated by some historians that from this early period dated his passion for the ill-starred Margaret Drummond, daughter of Lord Drummond—a father who was in no wise reluctant to permit her to become a King's mistress—and that when, in the course of the autumn, he accompanied the Lords Justices on their progress through the provinces, Margaret was his companion.

By October the first Parliament of the new reign had been called together, the leaders of the late King's party, who had fought in his defence, being summoned to appear and to answer to the charge of treason.

The meeting of that Parliament was a time of anxiety to not a few of those who attended it. Many of its members must have felt that their fate hung in the balances. The two factions stood over against one another, sworn foes. By their successful rivals, the men who had adhered to the dead King were branded as traitors to his son. The wording of their summons to Edinburgh had been a studied insult. Twenty-eight lords and a hundred and sixty great barons were bidden to appear before the King to answer for their " treasonable and cruel coming with the King's father against himself at Bannockburn ; thinking there to cause the father devour the son." On the other hand, in the eyes of the friends of the late sovereign, the rebels were steeped in treachery only the more black since they sheltered themselves under the name of his son. Lastly, between the two, stood James IV himself, with his ambitions, his hopes, his penitence, his remorse, and his accesses of melancholy, in some measure an uncertain element in the struggle for predominance. It was well to act promptly —so Angus and his comrades must have felt—

for who could tell what might befall when the boy, as yet an instrument in their hands, should have come to man's estate and taken the government of the realm upon himself? Would he show gratitude to the men who had set the crown upon his head ; or would he bear them a grudge for having led him to his throne over his father's grave ?

On the whole, matters were conducted with more moderation than might have been expected, nor do the dominant faction seem to have used their power unwisely. Buchan and Ross of Montgrenau, who had been attainted, made confession of guilt and received a free pardon. The late King's favourite, Ramsay—his present title of Earl of Bothwell appears to have been withdrawn at a later date —was treated with the like leniency. Their comrades were found guilty, and sentence of forfeiture was passed upon them, but no one was made to pay the death penalty, nor were rigorous measures taken against the malcontents.

In the proceedings of this first Parliament one scene stands out, when David, Lord Lindsay—the same who had presented the King with the charger on which he rode to his death—was brought to face his accusers.

If the encounter between him and his triumphant opponents was of less intrinsic importance than the space accorded to it in the
pages of his chronicler and namesake would
imply, and if, moreover, it may owe something to the imagination of the latter, it is
nevertheless a vivid presentment of what
may in substance have taken place.

When Lord Lindsay was called upon to
answer to the charge of treason preferred
against him no man of law was forthcoming
bold enough to incur the displeasure of the new
King, sitting in judgment, by undertaking his
defence ; and Lindsay's reply was a fierce
challenge to his foes, accompanied by the offer
to prove with his own hands upon any of them,
that it was they, and not he, who merited the
name of traitor. Turning upon his enemies,
passion carried him away and no fear of consequences availed to cause him to measure his
language, as he charged them with the murder
of the father and with having made of the son
the buckler of their wicked enterprise : " Therefore, if the King punish not you hastily for that
murder," he went on, " you will murder him
when you think time, as you did the father."
Then, addressing himself directly to the young

King: "Sir," he added, "beware of them and give them no credence, for they that were false to your father can never be true to yourself." Had his master lived he would still have taken his part and have feared no man. In the same way, should James have a son in revolt against him, he would fight in his quarrel better than the false traitors who had maligned him to the King.

In the end, in deference to a protest from Lindsay's brother, to the effect that, James being himself a party in the dispute, he was thereby disqualified in law from sitting in judgment upon it, or being present at the debate, the King was requested to withdraw, which he did, though reluctantly, "being a young Prince, sitting on his royal seat"— and Patrick Lindsay then proved, to the satisfaction of those present, that by an oversight the time for bringing his brother to justice had been allowed to expire, and the culprit was permitted to escape. James, possibly resenting his expulsion from the Council, sent the successful pleader to Bute for a year.

The late King's adherents having been dealt with, it was necessary for the opposite party to make their position and innocence clear ; which they accordingly did, by a declaration that, for the slaughter in the field at Stirling, "where our sovereign Lord's father happened to be slain," the dead man and his perverse Council were wholly to blame, the present King, his true lords and barons, being "innocent, white, and free of the same slaughter." The conclusion thus arrived at was eminently satisfactory to the majority by whom it was recorded, and the matter of the insurrection was dismissed.

It remained to make arrangements with regard to the future. Before the assembling of Parliament envoys had been despatched to England, and the truce of 1486 had been renewed with Henry VII. It was now determined that ambassadors should visit France, Burgundy, Austria, and other courts, carrying with them the declaration of the innocence of James and his counsellors, and should not only strive to establish peaceful relations with foreign Powers, but should seek for the King a wife who should be "a noble princess, born and descended from some worshipful house of ancient honour and dignity." No time was to be lost, so far as his guardians and counsellors

5

could compass it, in getting their young master married. But difficulties of more than one nature were to bar the way, and fifteen years passed before their desire was to find accomplishment.

CHAPTER V

1488—1495

Scottish malcontents—Sir Andrew Wood's sea-fights and victories—James's popularity—The Pope offers him consolation—Condition of the Highlands and the Isles —The administration of justice—The Lollards of Kyle —Question of the King's marriage—Margaret Drummond

JAMES was, to all appearances, securely established on the throne. His two little brothers were as yet scarcely of an age to be made use of, even as figureheads, by malcontent subjects. The contingency suggested by Lindsay, of a rebellious son, was still remote ; and the attempts at insurrection which were made proved vain. Lord Lennox and Lord Lyle, though partisans of James's in the struggle with his father, were discontented with the apportionment of spoil, and had headed a revolt, holding certain castles, including Dumbarton, against the King ; and in the north Lord Forbes had collected a force, and, using as his standard the bloody shirt of the murdered sovereign, refused to submit to the present Government. Neither insurrection, however, met with any lasting success and by the end of the year 1489 the country was, outwardly, at peace.

Nevertheless, the scenes which had marked James's accession could not fail to remain in men's minds, and it must have been felt that they might at any time afford grounds for disloyalty. To these early years must belong an undated letter addressed to Henry VII by the Master of Huntley which is proof of the smouldering disaffection of the nobles who had been faithful to the late King. Reminding Henry of the "treasonable and cruel slaughter of [his] sovereign Lord and King, falsely slain by a part of his false and untrue lieges," Huntley went on to state that he himself, with divers of his said sovereign's friends and kinsmen, had joined together to cause those guilty of the murder to be punished. "For the which I and the rest of my lords and fellows most humbly beseech your Grace to put to your hand . . . for the honour that every anointed prince and king should keep to others in the punishing of false and treasonable traitors. . . ."

Henry was not inclined at the moment to throw himself into a war in defence of the

monarchical system, and James IV continued
undisturbed in the possession of his kingdom.
Hostilities were as usual carried on in an
informal fashion between the belligerent
neighbours, and in these skirmishes success
chiefly belonged to the Scots. Sir Andrew
Wood, loyal servant as he had been to James III,
had been reconciled to the present Government, and in the course of the year 1489 was
the hero of two brilliant exploits.

The opportunity had been, in the first place,
afforded him by a raid of five English ships who
spread destruction in the Firth of Forth, all
merchantmen that could be laid hands on being
seized and robbed by the pirates. Confronted
by the necessity of taking vengeance on the
marauders, James and his Council found themselves in a difficulty. No sailors or mariners
could be induced to go to sea against them;
and in the end it was thought well to ignore
the past, to condone the attitude taken up
by Wood, offering to supply him with men
and artillery, with the further promise of rich
reward, on condition that he would consent to
undertake the adventure. It was a commission
much to Wood's liking; and with the famous
Yellow Carvell and the *Flower*, he sailed against

the English vessels, fought and conquered
them, and brought all five, with their captains,
in triumph to the King. Nor was this all ; for
later on, when Henry VII sent a certain Stephen
Bull to avenge the defeat of his countrymen,
another and a fiercer battle took place, lasting
through two long summer days, and resulting
in a second victory for Wood, who was again
able to place the English captain in the hands
of the King. With the generosity always a
feature of James's character, he not only
rewarded Sir Andrew, but also presented gifts
to the English sailors and sent them safely
home, because they "had shown themselves
so stout and hardy warriors," adding the
caution that should they come again they
might not be equally well entertained.

Meantime, as the years passed by, James
was winning golden opinions amongst all
classes of his subjects. In spite of his youth,
he had had a lesson in the effects and dangers
of misgovernment ; he never fell into his
father's fatal errors nor alienated the powerful
nobles by preferring to them lowborn flatterers
of his own creation.[1] The men who were fitted

---

[1] It was noteworthy that, throughout his reign, no man
could boast of holding the position of a favourite.

by position and birth to be his advisers were
accepted by him as such, and he was popular
amongst the nobility. On the other hand, he
would ride like a prince of romance in search
of adventure through the country, alone and
unattended, his rank unknown and lodging in
any houses he might chance to pass in the
character of a common wayfarer ; making
inquiries as he went concerning the King—
what manner of man he was, and how he was
spoken of in the realm ; and learning by this
means what was said of him by his subjects.

What he heard, even when his incognito had
been successfully preserved, would commonly
have proved to his liking. James was pre-
eminently a prince to win the love and loyalty
of his subjects, making his appeal alike to their
imagination and their heart. The characteristics of the ill-fated Stewarts were strongly
developed in his case, and the affection lavished
upon him, the submission yielded to his will,
even when it conflicted with that of his people
and with the better judgment of cooler-headed
men, testifies to his possession of the personal
attraction belonging to so many of his race.
In contrast to what had been considered the
parsimony of his father, his expenditure and his

liberality were profuse to extravagance. With a love of science and art, and especially of music, he combined a taste for knightly sports and was a bold rider. Notwithstanding the religious element developed in him to the point of superstition his court was a gay one. Tournaments, joustings, and trials of strength constantly took place, to which crowds would flock, amongst whom were knights from foreign countries, drawn to visit Edinburgh by reports of what was going forward there under the auspices of its young sovereign.

And yet, in spite of all, in spite of the distraction afforded both by attention to his duties and to affairs of State, and by amusement and pleasure, in spite of the versatility of his mind and his keen interest in every branch of knowledge, the shadow of the past lay heavily upon the King, making its presence felt at times to so marked a degree that it is said in the early days of his reign a warning was administered to him, to the effect that should he give himself up overmuch to sorrow —the sorrow that constituted a standing menace to the men to whom it was due—one of his brothers might be chosen to take his place. It was when matters were in this condition that

James the 4.th
King of Scotland.

messengers arrived from Pope Innocent VIII bearing missives addressed to the King and the nobles.

These documents were no doubt in tardy response to the justification of their proceedings despatched to the several courts of Europe by the men responsible for the events by which James's accession had been preceded. By a rescript addressed to the Abbots of Paisley and Jedburgh and to the Chancellor of the see of Glasgow, Innocent empowered these ecclesiastics to grant absolution to the persons, provided they were penitent, who had risen against the late King. By Andrew Forman, a papal pro-notary, destined to play an important part in Scottish affairs, a letter was brought, addressed to James himself.

To the young King consolation was offered. It may be that intimations of his state of mind had been conveyed to the Pope. In the present document it was taken for granted that, in the struggle with his father, James had been no more than the reluctant instrument of the will of men he was unable to control. This being the case, and having been unconsenting to the deed, he was free from the guilt attached to it. It was to those who had led him away that remorse and torture of conscience belonged, nor should he impute their wickedness to himself. Pitied by man for his father's disaster, so he would be pardoned by Heaven.

James may have derived what comfort he could from the papal letter ; but he was too clear-sighted and sincere to accept unreservedly the exculpation it contained, and he continued, in spite of it, to wear the iron belt significant of guilt and repentance.

In practical matters the new reign was to be marked by a strict administration of the law long absent from the realm. The need of reform is shown by incidents such as one belonging to the autumn of 1490, when James had been two years upon the throne. An ancient feud existing between the Murrays and the Drummonds, both dwellers in Perthshire, had broken out anew, and between one and two hundred of the Murrays had been shut up in a church by their successful opponents. As the latter marched away a shot was fired from the church, and one of the victors was slain ; whereupon, turning back, they set fire to the building in which their enemies were confined and burnt it to the ground. One only of the

Murrays escaped with his life.   That same year justice was done upon the ringleaders amongst the Drummonds, and they were executed at Stirling.

A more permanent source of uneasiness to the Scottish Government during these years was the condition of the western Highlands, which had been in a chronic state of revolt ever since, in 1461, John, Earl of Ross and Lord of the Isles, had arrogated to himself the position of an independent sovereign. As such he had entered into a secret treaty with Edward IV, always ready to foment Scottish disorder. For twelve years he had bidden defiance to James III, and it was not till peace with England had left him unsupported that he was compelled by force of arms to give in his submission. Nor was he even then treated with undue severity.   Though deprived of his earldom and of some of his other possessions, he was legally confirmed in the title of Lord of the Isles, and permitted to sit in Parliament in that capacity.   If it had been hoped to secure peace by leniency, such anticipations were signally disappointed ; nor did the submission of their chief carry with it that of his turbulent vassals. By his natural son, Angus, and later on by his nephew, Alexander of Lochalsh, the Government continued to be set at defiance. In May 1493 a decided step was taken and sentence of forfeiture was formally pronounced on the old rebel ; James in person visiting the scene of disorder and receiving the submission of several minor chieftains. John, aged and broken, had no alternative but to yield ; and it was hoped that peace might ensue at length.

Again that hope was destined to prove illusory. In July of the same year there was fresh trouble. The King had once more repaired to the disaffected districts, and had placed a garrison in Dunaverty Castle—Tarbut had been garrisoned some months earlier—with a view of overawing the surrounding country. The first effect was in an opposite direction. A native chief, John of Isla, considering the presence of royal troops in Dunaverty an outrage on his rights, stormed the castle under the very eyes of the King—who was on board the vessel that was to convey him back to the mainland— and hanged the governor over the wall. It was a bold and insolent defiance, nor was chastisement long delayed. Though powerless to intervene at the moment, James was not slow to avenge the insult offered to the royal dignity and to himself as its representative, and before many months had gone by John of Isla, his son, and his subordinate accomplices had paid the death penalty at Edinburgh.

During the following year, 1495, James was again present in the islands and took what measures were possible to reduce the recalcitrant chiefs to obedience. His success remained imperfect, and the struggle was for a time suspended, the differences with England by which he was occupied during the years 1496 and 1497 diverting his attention more or less from his domestic rebels and their intermittent attempts to revive their claim to *quasi* independence.

If the condition of the west supplied the most serious cause of uneasiness in the early years of James's reign, other matters had not been neglected. Justice was executed upon the robbers and thieves he had found abounding in the country, and the King personally concerned himself with the administration of the law. To spiritual questions he also gave his attention, and in the year 1494—he was twenty-two at the time—he presided over the trial of the Lollards of Kyle, who, to the number of thirty, were summoned to appear before King and

Council and answer to the charge of heresy preferred against them. Many of the accused—there were women amongst them—were friends of James's own, and the fact that his heart was inclined to gentleness, as was indeed usually the case, was considered one of the explanations of their ultimate escape.

Another reason may have been supplied by the ready wit of their chief spokesman, one Adam Reid, who took the line of varying his examination by the introduction of doggrel rhymes, turning what was a serious affair, if not one of life and death, into a farce.

To the Bishop's question, " Reid, believe ye that God is in heaven ? " he answered, " Not as I do the sacraments seven." "Whereat the Bishop, thinking to have triumphed, said, ' Sir, lo, he denies that God is in heaven.' Whereat the King wondering said, ' Adam Reid, what say ye ? ' The other answered, ' Please your Grace to hear the end between the churl and me.' "

Turning to the Bishop, he proceeded to vindicate his doctrines, adding the counter-charge against his accuser that he made himself checkmate to the King and forgot the injunction to preach the evangel and not to play the proud prelate, "as all the rabble of you do this day."

"And now, Sir," he ended, addressing James, "judge ye whether the Bishop or I believe best that God is in Heaven."

The young King appears to have had small desire to act as a theological censor and to have chiefly aimed at putting an end to the dispute. Would Reid, he asked, "burn his bill?"

"Sir, the Bishop and ye will," was Reid's reply.

"With these and the like scoffs the Bishop and his band were so dashed out of countenance that the greatest part of the accusation was turned to laughter," [1] and the culprits escaped.

It has been seen that from the time of his accession the question of James's marriage had been anxiously considered by those who administered the government during his minority. It had been anxiously considered all his life.

He must have been familiar from childhood with the names of the various princesses to whom he had been in turn allotted. Cecilia of England, as well as her cousin Anne, had each

---

[1] Knox's *History of the Reformation.*

borne his name at the English court. There had rarely been a time when his hand had not been offered as a bribe to some power it was desirable to conciliate. Nor would the question be allowed to rest now that he wore the crown of Scotland. But so far no decision had been taken.

James himself was not in haste to choose a wife. That each and all of the attempts to provide him with one had proved futile, and the familiarity with the situation thus engendered, may in part explain his acquiescence in preliminaries which, judging by the past, he might reasonably regard as unlikely to lead to serious results. He placed no obstacles in the way of the dispatch of embassies to the various courts of Europe with the ostensible object of providing him with a bride. It gave his Council pleasure to send them ; those with whom negotiations were opened might be flattered, and the arrangement of peaceful relations with the several powers facilitated. Should matters threaten to assume a graver and more practical aspect, a way of escape would not be hard to find. So James may conceivably have argued.

If the tale of his connection with the beautiful Margaret Drummond is founded on fact, some

explanation of this kind is necessary. That
Scotland remained without a Queen until
James was over thirty is negative evidence
in favour of a story said by some to have had
its beginnings in the days when he was still
Duke of Rothsay. His connection with Lord
Drummond's daughter is confirmed by actual
proof in the year 1497,[1] when she bore him
a daughter called by her name and lived openly
at Stirling Castle under the care of Lady
Lundy. A detailed account of the matter
was widely spread and may contain a certain
amount of truth. It was affirmed that so great
was his devotion that James had determined
to make Margaret his wife, and that pending the
arrival of the dispensation from Rome rendered
necessary by some distant blood-relationship, a
clandestine marriage had taken place before the
birth of their child. Should he have been bent
upon making her Queen it would further
explain the readiness with which it will be
seen that he entered upon negotiations with
Henry VII with reference to a marriage with
his daughter, then no more than a child. The

---

[1] The entries of items in the Treasurer's accounts which
are cited as evidence of an earlier date had reference merely
to Lady Margaret Stewart, aunt to the King.

6

demands of his people—who had voted a thousand pounds " for the honourable hame-bringing of a Queen," would be satisfied should a betrothal be arranged ; he would obtain a respite from pressure on the subject ; years would pass before the marriage could take place, and he may have trusted to time to provide a means of evading the obligations he had incurred. The knot was ultimately to be cut, after a fashion he had not contemplated, by Margaret's premature and tragic death.

In the meantime his attention was mainly centred upon an enterprise after his own heart. It was at this time that James pledged himself to support the claims of Perkin Warbeck, whose right to represent the House of York was a subject of interest throughout Europe. The spirit of chivalry, carried to excess, apparent throughout James's life, lent him a resemblance to the traditional knight-errant. To this spirit were due some of his greatest disasters ; and this quality, supplemented, it is true, by less disinterested motives, now enlisted him on the side of the vagrant adventurer who called himself Richard, Duke of York.

MARGARET OF DENMARK.
From an engraving by Harding after a painting by Jameson.

CHAPTER VI

1495

Perkin Warbeck, his past and his present—His arrival in
Scotland—Receives a royal welcome.

GIVEN James's character, his disposition and
his tastes, nothing was more natural than that
he should adopt Perkin Warbeck's cause.   That
its espousal would involve war was not likely
to deter him.   He loved fighting, and Henry
Tudor, in spite of the fitful endeavours at
reconciliation that had taken place, represented
the nation with which war had become a
Scottish habit and tradition.   The adoption
of the theory that the English throne was occupied by a usurper, to the detriment of the
rightful heir, set the ingrain race antagonism
on a higher plane and transformed hostility
into an act of justice.

For four years before his arrival in Scotland
the pretender had been in some measure before
the world.   Letters had passed between him

and James, and constant reports must have crossed the sea regarding the various adventures of the vagabond Prince—reports true and false, but alike serving to invest the wronged and dispossessed descendant of the house of York with the colours of romance.

The story began with his landing, a mere boy, in Ireland ; when the men of Cork—at first indeed in his own despite—had determined that the stranger was of the royal blood. Desmond had given him his support, and the Duchess of Burgundy, Edward IV's sister, endorsing the verdict of the Irish, had received him as her nephew and as rightful heir to her brother's kingdom. Afterwards Charles VIII, at war with Henry at the time, had summoned the lad to Paris and, treating him as a royal visitor, had given him a guard of honour, and malcontent Yorkists had crossed the Channel to join him. When Charles, making peace with England, had found it consort with his interests to dismiss his guest, Warbeck had not been left without support. The Emperor Maximilian, as well as the young Archduke Philip, were eager exponents of the claims of " the feigned lad " or " garçon," as Henry VII contemptuously

called him, their confidence in his identity
with the dead Richard lending importance to
what might have seemed a forlorn hope. Next
came the abortive expedition to Kent, where
the rough peasants, wholly incredulous of his
tale, had risen unanimously against those of
his followers who had ventured to land, had
defeated them unaided, and had dismissed
their leader with words of contempt. " As
for this fellow," they said of Warbeck, who had
prudently refrained from coming ashore till it
had been ascertained what species of reception
would be accorded him, " let him go back to
his father and mother, who live in France."

Gathering together, to use the language of
the English chronicler, [1] "his ungracious company," the adventurer determined upon a
second visit to Ireland, whence, with augmented
forces, the west of England might be made
a point of attack ; or, if this plan should
not be found feasible, Scotland might be
reached, " knowing that seldom or never is
perfect amity between the Scots and the English
nation." Another failure in Ireland followed ;
where, assisted by Desmond, he attempted in
vain the siege of Waterford ; and it was then

[1] Hall.

that " when the wind served him, he departed from Cork and arrived in Scotland."

The fact that he had been unfortunate would, to a man of James's temperament and character, serve rather as a recommendation than as a reason to turn the suppliant from his door ; and even before he had landed, preparations had been set on foot to give the wanderer a royal welcome at Stirling.

Already James had made it clear that he was not disinclined to lend the pretender his support. That same year, and before the two had been brought into personal relations, he had taken the step of sending an embassy to Maximilian, proposing to adopt Warbeck's cause, on condition that the Emperor would unite with Scotland against the English. The possibility of a combination of Maximilian and James against him may have moved Henry from the attitude of contempt he had maintained with regard to the claimant and have invested Warbeck with an importance he had lacked. If it is true, as some authorities state, that he made an endeavour at this time to conciliate James by the offer of his daughter's hand, the measure would indicate a disposition to take the matter more seriously than he had hitherto done. Nothing, however, had come of any negotiations that had taken place when, in November 1495, Warbeck arrived at Stirling.

What passed at the first interview between the King of Scots and his guest has been variously related, sometimes in bare and naked outline, sometimes with details which can scarcely fail to be attributed to the imagination of the narrator. It is certain that the adventurer was given no reason to regret the step he had taken in throwing himself upon the compassion of the traditional enemy of England.

The astonishing success achieved by Warbeck in establishing in so many quarters his identity with the heir of the house of York must have been due in some measure at least to personal qualities. The Duchess of Burgundy, hating Henry VII " even beyond the tenderness of her sex "—to use the language of an early and irate biographer—may have prepared him to act his part, have instructed him in the history of his reputed family, have taught him the usages and language of royalty. But there must have been something more to explain the impression made by the adventurer upon all sorts and conditions of men, from the rough Irish peasants to emperors and kings.

His beauty and grace, the dignity with which he sustained his difficult part, became a legend to be handed down. "Of visage beautiful," wrote one of his fiercest biographers in 1618, " of countenance majestical, of wit subtle and crafty, in education pregnant, in languages skilful, of behaviour extraordinary, and of manners audacious." [1]   All this will have taken its effect upon his young host—not more than twenty-two at the time—and if the personal charm of the wanderer was calculated to appeal to James, the cause he was invited to further was precisely one to gratify his spirit of adventure.

And what was Perkin Warbeck himself ? What was the man underneath his disguise ?

In the face of the evidence brought together by modern research, of the corroboration of his last confession supplied by independent facts, and of the letter to his mother printed by James Gairdner, it is difficult to admit the possibility—of which Walpole was the most prominent supporter—that Warbeck was in truth the man he claimed to be.   But between accepting this hypothesis and dismissing him

[1] Thomas Gainsford, *The True and Wonderfull History of Perkin Warbeck.*

PERKIN WARBECK.
From a contemporary drawing.

as a mere skilful cheat and trickster, there is
a middle course : it may be questioned whether
he was not partly and at some periods his
own dupe. It should be remembered that
when the men of Cork first forced his royalty
upon him, he was no more than a boy, and
that at that time he showed no disposition to
accept the offered dignity. That he was the son
of Clarence he denied upon oath, also rejecting
the suggestion that he was a bastard of Richard
III. Nor was it until, obstinate in their
determination to discover in him a representative of the White Rose, his entertainers in-
sisted that he was Richard of York, does he
seem to have resigned himself to play the
part assigned him, on the assurance that he
need not fear, since they were determined to
be revenged on Henry. "And so, against
my will, they made me learn English, and taught
me what I should do and say."

So runs the confession—genuine or false,
dictated by Henry or voluntary, who can tell ?

Since then years had passed ; nor is it
beyond the bounds of possibility that, welcomed
by the Duchess of Burgundy as her nephew,
flattered and dazzled by the position accorded
him, he may have insensibly drifted into the

belief that the tale that was taught him was not wholly false. Human nature is many-sided; and in the stress and excitement of the life he was leading, the early years of childhood, to which had quickly succeeded a period of travel, may have assumed the character of a dream, and he may insensibly have become his part. It is difficult to believe that he could have brought to it such consistency, so much kingly grace and dignity, had he throughout and at every moment been conscious that he was in truth no more than a common trickster and impostor.

Such as they were, the two men now met face to face, King and adventurer, diamond and paste; and if the description of the interview supplied by Buchanan may not adhere closely to fact, it probably gives a sufficiently correct impression of what took place, corroborated as it is by entries in the Treasurer's accounts concerning arras work taken from Edinburgh to Stirling to lend magnificence to the occasion, of raiment bought for "the Prince," and other indications that James was determined from the first to treat his guest as if his pretensions had been sifted and acknowledged.

Admitted that November day to the royal presence, the adventurer rehearsed the tale that must by this time have been familiar to him. He lamented the ruin of the house of York and earnestly entreated help. As they confronted one another, the one upon his throne, the other a homeless vagrant, youth appealed to youth, and all the chivalry in James's nature will have lent force to that appeal. Replying in words of encouragement, he introduced Warbeck to his Council and caused him there to repeat his story of misfortune—pathetic enough, had it been true. Such and so great had been the misery he had endured that, in comparison, he declared that he accounted his murdered brother happy. Yet he was not so broken in spirit as to give up hope ; and should success attend his efforts he would show what a friend Scotland had acquired in him.

James's answer was kind if undecisive. The question, he said, must be referred to his Council. One promise he made. Whatever might be their conclusion, he assured his guest that he should never repent having sought refuge with him. He kept his word.

CHAPTER VII

1495—1496

Warbeck at Court—His marriage—Ferdinand and Isabella
and their diplomatic methods—Letters of Sir John
Ramsay to Henry VII—His accounts of James's court
and of Warbeck—Concressault, the French envoy
—Plots—The border crossed by James—Failure of the
expedition.

THUS opened the fresh chapter in Perkin
Warbeck's history. It was soon clear that the
object which had brought him to Scotland—
that of enlisting its King upon his side—had
been fully attained. The more level-headed
and cautious amongst his counsellors might
regret James's rashness ; but, as a keen observer
noted, though he did not refuse to listen to the
arguments of his advisers, it was his custom
to settle important questions for himself ; and
on this occasion, overriding all objections, he
lost no time in pronouncing in favour of the
claims of the refugee, took him on royal pro-
gresses about the country, called him cousin,
displayed him to the populace as Richard, Duke

of York, and, further, " sealing both his own eyes and the eyes of the world," gave him in marriage—a conclusive proof of his confidence—the hand of his kinswoman, Lady Katherine Gordon, noted for her beauty and daughter of the Earl of Huntley.

The adventurer may well have been dazzled by his success. What Lady Katherine's sentiments were at this time nothing remains to show ; but the sequel proves that Warbeck had not failed to win his wife's heart, and that she was ready to follow his fortunes, good or ill, wherever they might lead her. A letter is extant, couched in the extravagant language of the day, addressed by the young man to the noble lady who was his promised wife. All, wrote the lover, turned their eyes to her, all admired, loved, and obeyed her ; and, struck by her rather divine than human beauty, believed her not to be born at that day, but to be descended from heaven. " All look at your face, so bright and serene that it gives splendour to the cloudy sky ; all look at your eyes, as brilliant as stars, which make all pain to be forgotten and turn despair into delight ; all look at your neck which outshines pearls, at your fine forehead, your purple light of youth, your fair hair, in one word, at the splendid perfection of your person, and looking at, they cannot choose but admire you ; admiring, they cannot choose but love you ; loving, they cannot choose but obey you. I shall, perhaps, be the happiest of all your admirers, and the happiest man on earth, since I have reason to hope that you will think me worthy of your love. . . . Whether waking or sleeping, I cannot find rest or happiness except in your affection. All my hopes rest in you, and in you alone. . . . Farewell, my soul and my consolation. You brightest ornament of Scotland, farewell, farewell."

Such is the document that has been preserved amongst Spanish papers. It may be that it was not displeasing to the writer's betrothed. Whilst his love-making went on, the news, spread abroad, of James's adoption of his cause occasioned a certain amount of disturbance in Europe. Henry VII could not fail to regard his conduct as tantamount to a declaration of war, and was naturally both indignant and uneasy at the additional importance thus conferred on the lad whose pretensions he had hitherto affected to treat with derision. Ferdinand and Isabella, too, anxious to maintain the balance of power which would be imperilled should France and Scotland join hands against Henry, took the step, in April 1496, of sending an embassy to Scotland with the object of averting that danger if possible. At Warbeck's claims they scoffed. " As for him who calls himself Duke," they wrote contemptuously to their envoy in England, " we hold it for a jest." It had occurred to them, as to others at an earlier date, that the offer of Margaret Tudor's hand might be a means of detaching James from the cause of the claimant, but her father appears to have dismissed the idea and to have rejected the suggestion on the score of the child's age. When he subsequently acted upon it, it was to no immediate purpose.

It is to be noted that the reference to Warbeck as " him of York," which occurs in another letter of the Spanish sovereigns, tends to belie the conviction they professed that he was an impostor. Impostor or not—a question of minor importance—there could be no doubt as to the genuineness of their desire that James could be induced to withdraw his support from him, and that he should continue on amicable terms with the present occupant of the English throne.

To James, for his part, though pledged to lend his assistance to Warbeck, an alliance with Spain presented certain attractions; and it would appear that, resorting to the usual expedient in such cases, he had vaguely suggested that it might be made to include a marriage between himself and some Spanish princess. In point of fact no princess existed available for the purpose, the Infanta Katharine, Ferdinand and Isabella's sole legitimate daughter, being already allotted to Prince Arthur, heir to the English throne. But in northern latitudes some uncertainty seems to have prevailed on this head—a confusion that Ferdinand and Isabella were in no haste to dispel. The methods they used in dealing with the young King are fully set forth in a letter addressed about this time to their envoy in England:

"It is as true as God is truth"—so this missive ran—"that we have no other purpose in our negotiations with Scotland than to win over the King of Scots and to make him friends with the King of England, so that he may no longer show favour to him of York or enter into an alliance with France"—which last was the real cause that prompted their intervention. "At all events we intend to put him off some time longer with vain hopes."

The idea of an Infanta who did not exist was to be kept in the King's mind and he was to be flattered and dazzled by the prospect of so brilliant an alliance and a problematical match never intended to prove more than a subject for discussion and evasion. "We have no daughter to give the King of Scots, as you well know," the Spanish sovereigns wrote to their envoy with shameless candour. . . . "You must tell this only to the King of England. . . . We must not deprive the King of Scots of his hope of having our daughter."

The reason of the deception was not far to seek. A solemn promise had been obtained from James that he would take no active measures in Warbeck's favour until his ambassadors had visited Spain and returned thence; and the aim of Spanish diplomacy was consequently to protract the negotiations, and to continue to make James their dupe: "We must amuse him as long as possible." In the meantime King Henry might offer the King of Scotland the hand of a daughter of his own.

Notwithstanding all this, James's preparations for an expedition into England, to be undertaken on Warbeck's behalf, had been carried forward, and by the early autumn of 1496, when the pretender had been nearly ten months in Scotland, they were complete. The guest was confident, in spite of his repulse in Kent, that he had merely to show himself in Northumberland to create a rising in his favour. Nor was his confidence altogether without justification. Not only had adherents collected around him abroad, but in 1493 a rising had taken place in his name in the North, and though it had been quelled without difficulty, it was in some sort proof of disaffection in that quarter.

Besides this, not a few of the northern nobles, Dacre, Heron, and others, were stealing across the Border to pay their homage to the man they accepted as the representative of the White Rose, undeterred by the fact that by so doing they were imperilling their lives or by the recollection of the deaths on the scaffold of some of those who had adopted the cause of the adventurer before them.

Taking for granted the belief of these men in his birth and in the justice of his claims, they could scarcely be accused of treason. If, on the contrary, they were making him a tool to be used against a King they disliked and were for that purpose playing into the hands of their country's enemies, there were Scots who, showing that England had no monopoly of treachery, were doing their best to make the balance even. At the very moment that James —having laid his plans and ridden in person through the country for the purpose of super-intending his preparations for the coming campaign—was on the point of entering England at the head of his army, traitors at his side kept a close watch upon his movements and despatched secret information concerning them to Henry.

At this juncture, and thanks to a correspond-ent of the English King, the mist that veils the past lifts for a moment and leaves King, court, and surroundings disclosed in sharp relief. The showman is John Ramsay, *alias* Earl of Both-well—by some the title was denied him and it was afterwards dropped and conferred upon Patrick Hepburn — James III's sometime favourite, now pardoned, received, and, at least, tolerated by James's son ; and acting at his court as Henry VII's confidential agent. The picture is contained in letters addressed to his patron, and the principal figures included in it are clearly sketched.

That of greatest interest is naturally the King, excited at the near prospect of the warlike enterprise upon which he is bent, his " young adventurousness " firing his blood, a noble object in view, a wrong to be redressed, justice to be done to the dispossessed heir of a royal line, and James himself to be the doer of it. Warbeck too is young—he is generally alluded to as " the boy " ; eager and hopeful, he makes terms and conditions with his allies as if he in truth occupied the English throne. Around these two central figures are grouped a crowd of Scottish nobles, too wise to approve what is in contemplation, yet loving their young King too well to thwart him ; and perhaps, as the time to take the field draws near, feeling the soldier's spirit awaken within them, making a fight, in a bad cause or a good, and especially when it is to be with their ancient enemy, no unwelcome prospect. And, lastly, the narrator is always present, a watchful and sinister observer of all that goes on, taking his notes with elaborate care, brooding over his past wrongs, of which the memory now and again betrays itself in the fierce expression of his longing that vengeance may overtake the man he hates ;

and awaiting his opportunity to strike a blow at his late master's son.

Already he had made an attempt to carry out his purpose, and had been involved, in 1491, in a treasonable conspiracy, in conjunction with the Earl of Buchan and Sir Thomas Tod. Had it been successful the King and his brother were to have been delivered over into English hands. The plot had failed, and Ramsay's share in it remaining undetected, he had continued at James's court, ready to render what service he could to his English employer. On September 6th, 1496, ten months after Warbeck's arrival at Stirling, he was sending a detailed account to Henry of the events then taking place with regard to the expedition in contemplation in aid of Warbeck.

He had, he assured his correspondent, laboured to do him service ; had solicited the King and all the well-advised Lords to desist from giving their support to the pretender and to make peace with England. His efforts, however, had proved vain, and in a week James, at the head of his army, was expected to be within ten miles of the English border, accompanied by Warbeck and his followers, 1,400 men of all nationalities—a motley troop.

It was probably true that, as the spy affirmed, almost all the barons, as well as the commoner people, disapproved of the project ; but protests were vain ; " this simple wilfulness cannot be removed out of the King's mind by no persuasion or means. I trust verily," adds the traitor fiercely, with one of his sudden bursts of passion, " that he will be punished, by your means, for the cruel consent of the murder of his father."

Coming to particulars, Ramsay related that on September 2nd James had held a council, Warbeck being present, when the terms on which he was to receive assistance had been discussed ; and it had been finally agreed, though not until the following morning, that should the projected expedition prove successful, Berwick was to be relinquished to Scotland, and the sum of fifty thousand marks was to be paid, within two years, towards the costs of the war.

Close upon this agreement with Warbeck had come the reception of Concressault, a French envoy. It was not the first time that he and Warbeck had met. When, early in his career, Charles VIII had sent for the boy to Paris, to be employed as an instrument against

Henry, the French noble accredited to the Scottish court had commanded the guard of honour placed about the young adventurer. The two had parted when Warbeck, no longer of use, had been summarily dismissed from France; they now met under changed circumstances, Concressault being sent by his master, ostensibly to mediate between Scotland and England and consequently to use his endeavours to blast the hopes of his late charge. He may have been instructed to be half-hearted in the business; he may also have had a lingering kindness for his former acquaintance. For Ramsay found him sorely deficient in zeal in the execution of his mission; and after James, in the presence of his Council, had given an account of the provocation he had received from England—of vessels burnt and cattle plundered—the French envoy seems to have allowed himself to be convinced that war was the natural and inevitable result of these misdoings: " After this the Lord Concressault was but right soft in the solicitation of this peace, and to mine appearance made but little diligence therein; saying to myself, after I desired him to make diligence, it was no wonder the King was stirred to unkindness."

If it was true, as was stated, that Concressault had been commissioned to offer a price for the possession of the person of the pretender, it indicated not a little ignorance on the part of the French King of the nature of the man with whom he had to deal. One hundred thousand crowns—the sum mentioned by Ramsay—would not have tempted James to traffic with his honour and send his guest to France, for what purpose the spy confessed himself ignorant. On the whole Ramsay expressed his belief that the coming of the French envoy had done but little good, " for he and the boy are every day in council."

It is evident that Ramsay himself looked forward not without satisfaction to an expedition to England certain, in his opinion, to result in disaster. " If it be not that your Grace pass in agreement with the King of Scots as meseems ye need little, and your Grace understood all things, I doubt not the young adventurousness of the King will both jeopardise himself, the boy, and all his people. And will your Grace do after my simple advertisement, I doubt not that journey shall be repented in Scotland this hundred year to come ; and by God Himself there shall not be in England shall more

willingly and truly help thereto [than himself] ;
because I find him so far out of reason, and so
little inclined to goodness, but all to trouble
and cruelty, without his will be fulfilled in all
points ; and were he once well snybbit, he
would be the better for it while he lives. . . ."
For a time Ramsay had been desirous of peace ;
now he inclines to a contrary opinion, a significant sentence betraying the animus of the
writer—" there is many of his father's servants
would see a remedy of the death of his
father. . . ."

Noting with satisfaction the absence of the
money which was so necessary a factor if a
war were to be carried to a successful issue,
Ramsay observed that James was very short
of cash. He did not possess a hundred pounds,
and was coining chains and plate to provide
it—making the people ill content.

The Duchess of Burgundy, kept well informed of what was to be attempted, had
sent what assistance she could, and the same
correspondent gave Henry an account of the
arrival of her envoy, Roderic de Lalane. " I
stood by when the King received him," he
relates, " in presence of Perkin, and thus he
said in French : ' Sir, I am come here according

to my promise to do your Highness service, and for none other man's sake am I come here ; for I had not had your letters of warrant, I had been arrested in Flanders and put to great trouble for Perkin's sake.' And he came not near Perkin ; and then came Perkin to him, and he saluted him, and asked how his aunt did ; and he said well : and he enquired if he had any letters from her to him, and he said he durst bring none, but he had to the King. And surely he has brought the King sundry pleasant things for the war, both for man and horse."

The manner of Lalane's accost, if correctly described, cannot have given Warbeck satisfaction ; and it would seem that the Duchess's convictions with regard to his identity with her lost nephew were not shared by her representative.

The help sent by his mistress—a small body of men and two ships—was doubtless welcome. However insufficiently provided with the sinews of war, and great as might be the risk he incurred in entering upon a struggle with England, James was bent, in his " simple wilfulness," upon fulfilling the promises made to his vagabond guest. Warbeck was to be

given one more chance of justifying his boast
that, once on English soil, the people would be
ready and eager to hail their rightful King,
and to show their loyalty to the White Rose.

Of the disapproval, silent though it might be,
of many of James's subjects, he can scarcely
have been unaware. He is not likely to have
had any suspicion of the degree to which
treachery was carried. It is clear that Ramsay
had an accomplice in his old fellow-conspirator
Buchan, whose resentment had been no more
softened than Ramsay's own by the indulgence
the King had accorded to both. In a later
letter written by the traitor from the Scottish
camp there is evidence that the two were again
engaged in some plot at Henry's bidding.
"My Lord of Buchan takes upon him the
fulfilling of it, if it be possible, and thinks best
now, in the long night within his tent, to enterprise the matter, for he has no watch but the
King's appointed to be about him. . . . I put
my Lord your letter, of the which he was full
glad and well content."

Ramsay himself had been tampering with
James's young brother. "I passed to St.
Andrews," he wrote, "and communed at length
with the King's brother and gave him the

cross-bow. He commends his services humbly to your Grace, and says he intends to do your Grace service ; and will not for aught the King can do come to this host against your Grace. And now my Lord of Murray passes over to him . . . and my Lord will solicit this young prince to come to your Grace."

The letter must have been written on the very eve of the expedition to which Ramsay was looking forward with hope and confidence. It is noticeable, nevertheless, that he twice expresses his opinion that if James could " have his mind fulfilled after our last communing with the Bishop of Durham " war might still have been avoided. It is difficult to see how this could have been done without involving a breach of the promises made to Warbeck. Nor is Ramsay a trustworthy authority on the subject of James's intentions and purposes.

Meantime, scouts had been sent over the Border to reconnoitre the condition of the country and had returned with encouraging reports. All was quiet, nor would it appear that any precautions were taken by the inhabitants to resist an attack. Such being the case, the time for an invasion would be well chosen ; and by September 20th the Scottish army was accordingly on English soil. As he marched, proclamations were issued by James, and pardon was promised to all who would take part with Richard, Duke of York, and would fight in his quarrel. In a further manifesto put forth by Warbeck, Henry was held up to reprobation as a usurper, and was likewise declared guilty of having infringed the liberties of the Church and oppressed the people by unjust taxation. These wrongs Warbeck pledged himself to redress, promising to maintain the rights and privileges of nobles and ecclesiastics. Finally he placed a reward of a thousand pounds on King Henry's head.

It is easy to imagine the anxiety with which the adventurer and his allies must have watched the effect of these proclamations and the bitterness of their disappointment at the total absence of response. It may be that the English apathy, if not hostility, has been rightly explained by traditional jealousy of Scotland, and that even the disaffected amongst the Northumbrian commoners would have been reluctant to accept a King imposed upon them by their ancient enemies. From whatever cause, they remained obstinately quiescent. It was clear that the support upon which Warbeck had so confidently counted was not to be forth-coming.

What followed may have been in part the result of disappointment ; in part it was in accordance with the usage of the times. The expedition which had started with the dignity of an invasion designed to dethrone a usurper and vindicate the claims of the rightful heir, quickly degenerated into a mere exaggerated border raid. The country was wasted and plundered, towns were burnt, the inhabitants slaughtered by the mixed forces, Scottish and foreign, under James's command. Since success was not to attend the enterprise, spoil and vengeance were made to replace it ; until Warbeck was moved to intercede on behalf of the unhappy people he affected to regard as his subjects, "beseeching the Scottish King that from thence-forth he would not afflict and plague his people." No power, he said, was so dear to him that he would desire that it should be purchased by their blood.

His show of compassion may have been sincere. Whether genuine or not, James was in no mood to be moved by it.

" Sir," he answered, " methinketh you take much pain and very much imagine how to pre-

serve the realm of another Prince which is
not yours ; but my mind giveth me that you
be far from obtaining the same." Not one
man had come forward, in the country he
called his own, to help in the war begun in his
name.

The youth of the speaker and the pressure of
disappointment, sharply felt, may excuse the
taunt ; but it was not the moment to throw
failure in the teeth of his companion in misfortune.

It was evident that no more could be done
at present to press Warbeck's claims. It may
even be, as one of the chroniclers avers, that
from this time there had arisen a doubt
in the King's mind as to the "young fond
foundling" whose cause he had so eagerly
embraced, and whose pretensions were stub-
bornly disallowed by those he called his countrymen. For the present there was nothing to do
but to acknowledge defeat ; and the Scottish
army marched home, laden with booty and
with the certain prospect of suffering an English
revenge.

Cooler than his antagonist, Henry bided
his time ; called Parliament together, and
obtained from it the supplies necessary for

making war upon those who—as the royal commission declared—had invaded England with an army of rebels and without commiseration of age or sex, had killed, plundered, seized fortresses, and given villages to the flames.

CHAPTER VIII

1496—1500

So far as Scotland was concerned, the champion-
ship of Warbeck's cause was practically ended
by the raid of September. Short as was the
time occupied by the expedition, it had conclusively demonstrated the vanity of his anticipations of effective support from the English
people. James may or may not have adhered to
the belief that his guest was the man he pur-
ported to be ; he had plainly renounced the
hope of placing him upon the English throne.
To surrender Perkin to his enemies was a
different matter ; and this, in spite of the
pressure brought to bear upon him, James
firmly refused to do. Kings were not credited
in those days with a high or scrupulous sense

of honour, and besides the generous bribe said
to have been offered by Charles VIII should
the pretender be delivered into his hands,
Henry would also have been ready to pay
well for the possession of his person ; but he
remained in safety at the Scottish court, treated
as beseemed his assumed rank, until the
middle of the following year. Though the
chronicler declares that the King, his host,
" every day more and more neglected and less
fancied and gave credit to him," it was not
until July 1497 that he asked him to find
another domicile.

Many reasons may have contributed to
prompt the request. Whether or not Warbeck
was the rightful heir to the English throne, it
was impossible, after all that had passed and
the countenance that had been shown him, to
treat him as other than the Duke of York ;
and the entertainment of a visitor of nominally
royal blood for an indefinite period was a
serious drain upon the resources of a treasury
ever in danger of being exhausted. A monthly
allowance made to Warbeck himself, together
with board and lodging for the English refugees
who had gathered about him, constituted a
heavy item in the Treasurer's accounts ; whilst

—a graver matter—his presence in Scotland rendered peace with England impossible, and was a standing cause of irritation to Henry.

Hitherto, it was true, insurrections and troubles at home had kept the latter too busy to leave him free to turn his attention, save in fitful fashion, northwards. Yet so long as no definite basis of agreement had been arrived at, it must have been well understood that he was merely waiting his time and that the recent attack would not ultimately be permitted to go unpunished. A species of guerilla warfare, kept up upon the Border, was an earnest of what might be expected when leisure and opportunity served.

In his more reasonable moments James can scarcely have failed to concur with the level-headed in both countries in recognising the desirability of peace. Nevertheless, sore from his recent defeat, he was in no conciliatory mood. He meant to treat a peace and not to go a-begging for one—so he declared through the Scottish Commissioners who met Fox, the Bishop of Durham, for the purpose of discussing possible terms of pacification. To Henry's initial demand that Warbeck should be handed over to him there could be only one reply. In vain the Bishop urged that the adventurer was no more than a fiction, and such a one that if a poet had projected his figure it could not have been done more to admiration—that he was a mere "pageant King." It might be true. James might, moreover, be growing to suspect it ; but the Bishop of Glasgow, answering on his behalf, though admitting that he was no competent judge of the young man's claims, made it clear that, having received him as a suppliant, accorded him protection, and wedded him to his kinswoman, it was a thing impossible that James should betray into the hands of his enemies the fugitive who had taken sanctuary in his realm.

He could not, however, be permitted to remain there, a permanent cause of discord. Even James acknowledged that the duty of hospitality had its limits, and that it was time that Perkin should go. Before the middle of July the intimation had been conveyed to him, and he was made aware that he must leave Scotland and seek an asylum elsewhere. The question suggests itself whether, driven from country to country, the "pageant King" may not have been growing weary of sustaining the burden of the greatness thrust upon him in the first instance unsought. But if it had been so, to break free from the meshes woven by a fraud of long standing can only be done by an effort of which few men would be capable, and Warbeck continued to act his part with consistency. James too maintained to the end of their relationship the attitude he had taken up, and the wanderer was dismissed without any slackening of the respect due to royalty.[1] The opportunity for his departure was taken whilst the King was absent across the English border ; a vessel was equipped, and Warbeck and his wife, still in the characters of Duke and Duchess of York, were escorted to Ayr, and there placed on board the ship which was to carry them to " a more convenient place of exile." According to Bacon, Perkin played his part well to the last, saying " that he saw his time was not yet come, but whatever his fortunes were he should always think and speak honourably of his Scottish Majesty." As no doubt he had cause to do.

---

[1] Mr. Gairdner considers it an open question whether, even at this date, James had abandoned the intention of assisting Warbeck to establish his claim.

Thus the adventurer and his wife took leave of the country where he had found shelter and hospitality for a year and eight months. In Scotland they were seen no more ; and at a time when news from foreign lands was hard to come by and uncertain, they had perhaps been almost forgotten when, thirteen years later, the recollection of what had become an old story was unexpectedly and curiously revived. It was some time in 1510, when the vagabond pretender had long paid the price of his adventure, that " a fair woman," calling herself Katharine Gordon and personating his wife, made her appearance in the country. Received with cordiality by the friends of the Earl of Huntley, her claim to be his daughter does not seem to have been disputed until, having ventured to approach the King himself, and possibly perceiving that her tale failed to carry conviction to his mind, she took the wiser part of making secret confession of her fraud and was by him dismissed from the country.[1]

With Warbeck's departure and James's practical abandonment of his cause, one difficulty in the way of a peace with England was removed. For the present any such pacification

---

[1] Bishop Lesley's *History of Scotland.*

appeared as far off as ever. James, smarting
from his recent reverses, seemed to be, on the
contrary, bent upon widening the breach between the two countries, and was once more
laying waste the English border, burning and
destroying wherever he went. Though Henry,
on the other hand, preoccupied by domestic
troubles, was becoming more and more disposed
to regard the marriage that took place six years
later as the best solution of the difficulties
attending Anglo-Scottish relations, James had
so far received the suggestion coldly. This
year—1497—his little daughter by Margaret
Drummond was born, and he may have been
indulging the hope that he would find it possible
to place the woman he loved on the throne.
However slow Henry had been to make reprisals, it was clear that he could not continue to
permit the northern provinces to be devastated
with impunity ; and the time came when it
was necessary to take measures to put an end
to the existing state of things. James was
laying siege to Norham Castle when tidings
that the Earl of Surrey, with a force superior
to his own, was close at hand, forced him to
retire hastily to Scottish ground, whither he
was quickly pursued by the Earl, who in his

turn laid the country waste, destroyed Cold-
stream Castle, with other strong places, and
finally forced the important fortress of Aytoun
to surrender under James's very eyes, so that
the smoke of the burning buildings could be
seen from his camp.

It was at this juncture that the King gave
yet another proof of the " young adventurousness " Ramsay had named as one of his characteristics. To Surrey, fresh from his success
at Aytoun, he sent heralds with a singular
proposal ; challenging the Earl either to bring
out his whole army to meet the royal troops
in fair fight, or suggesting as an alternative
that they two, James himself and the English
commander in chief, should meet " person to
person and hand to hand," in single combat,
on condition that, should the King be victor,
the town and castle of Berwick should constitute
Surrey's ransom. It does not appear what was
to take place should James suffer defeat ; nor
does the possibility of either combatant being
slain outright seem to have been contemplated.

Surrey, in reply, chose the first alternative.
As to the King's second suggestion, whilst
thanking him heartily for the honour he had
done him in offering to fight so poor an Earl

body to body, he pointed out that Berwick belonged to the King his master, and not to him, nor could he venture it as the stake. His own body he would willingly put in pledge, though it was more precious to him than all the towns in the world. Should he chance to take the King prisoner, he would forgo his share of the ransom ; paying, in case he was vanquished, the sum due for an earl.

Nothing came of the negotiations. Berwick was what James wished to fight for, and Berwick could not be risked on an uncertain hazard ; the affair therefore only resulted in emphasising James's reckless and chivalrous daring, of which Surrey's experience was to stand him in good stead when once again the two stood over against each other as mortal enemies.

According to the English chronicler, naturally biassed in favour of his countrymen, the King, finding his conditions were declined, suddenly fled by night. He may have thought it well to leave the enemy to struggle alone with the natural forces arrayed against them, and the event proved him right. For, the Scottish army gone, and Surrey being " daily and nightly vexed with continual wind and immeasurable rain, he could not cause his people to con-

tinue in that tempestuous and barren region,"
and retreating to Berwick, he disbanded his
forces.

The belligerents being now quits, and a proper
and reasonable amount of suffering having been
inflicted on the unoffending dwellers on either
side of the Border, the two Kings took into
serious consideration the advisability of making
peace; and James seems to have come, gradually and reluctantly, to the conclusion that
he could not afford to refuse the bait held out,
in a marriage with Margaret Tudor, to induce
him to forgo his favourite occupation of making
war.

There was little in the arrangement to tempt
him personally to relinquish his freedom in
accepting as his wife a child of nine years old.
On the other hand, the eldest daughter of the
King of England was a match which, in his
public character, he could not hope to better;
and though nothing was as yet definitely concluded, it was plain that all tended towards the
accomplishment of the union.

It has been seen that Spain, with an eye to
her own interests, had been already genuinely
anxious to promote an understanding which
would serve to detach James from the ancient

Prince Henry   Prince Arthur   Princess Margaret

THE CHILDREN OF HENRY VII.

From an engraving by G. Vertue after the painting by Mabuse.

122]

ally of Scotland, France, and she now again intervened with this object.

Ayala, the envoy sent from Madrid, was eminently fitted to accomplish his purpose. During the previous year he had visited Edinburgh, in order to persuade James, had it been possible, to abandon the cause of the English pretender. He would seem, in the course of his mission, to have become attached to the young King and to have gained his confidence ; and at the present juncture he was once more an agent at the Scottish Court.   A keen and shrewd observer, he was recognised as an authority on Scottish affairs ; the Spanish envoys in London writing to Ferdinand and Isabella in July 1498 that they " could get no information respecting Scotland save from Don Pedro de Ayala, who is staying in London in order to recruit his health. . . . He knows England well, but Scotland better. He is, in fact, the only man who knows Scotland, all others looking on the Scots as their enemies and flying into a passion as soon as the name of Scotland is pronounced." The writers added that they had requested Don Pedro to send an account of England and Scotland to Spain.

To this suggestion is due the most detailed

description extant of James as he then was, at the age of twenty-five—one worth quoting at length, as the result of observations carried on for some two years.

" He is of noble stature," wrote the Spaniard, " neither tall nor short, and as handsome in complexion and shape as a man can be. His address is very agreeable. He speaks the following languages : Latin, very well ; French, German, Flemish, Italian and Spanish ; Spanish as well as the Marquis, but he pronounces it more distinctly. . . . His knowledge of languages is wonderful. He is well read in the Bible and in some other devout books. He is a good historian. He has read many Latin and French histories and profited by them, as he has a very good memory. He never cuts his hair or his beard.[1] It becomes him very well. He fears God and observes all the precepts of the Church. He does not eat meat on Wednesdays and Fridays. He would not ride on Sundays for any consideration—not even to Mass. He says all his prayers. He hears two Masses before transacting any business. After

[1] It is conjectured by some that this only signifies that his beard was not close clipped. The engravings represent him as shaven.

Mass he has a cantata sung, during which he sometimes dispatches very urgent business. He gives alms liberally, but is a severe judge, especially in the case of murderers. He has a great predilection for priests, especially for the Friars Observant, with whom he confesses. Rarely, even in jesting, a word escapes him that is not the truth. He prides himself much upon it, and says it does not seem to him well for Kings to swear their treaties, as they do now. The oath of a King should be his royal word, as was the case in bygone ages. . . . He is courageous, even more than a King should be. I am a good witness of it. I have often seen him undertake most dangerous things in the late wars. I sometimes clung to his skirts, and succeeded in keeping him back. On such occasions he takes not the least care of himself. He is not a good captain, because he begins to fight before his orders have been given. He told me that his subjects serve him with their person and goods in quarrels just and unjust, exactly as he likes, and that therefore he does not think it right to begin any warlike undertaking without being himself the first in danger. His deeds are as good as his words. For this reason and because he is a very humane prince, he is greatly loved. He is active and works hard. When he is not at war he hunts in the mountains. I tell your Highnesses the truth when I say that God has worked a miracle in him, for never out of Spain have I seen a man so temperate in eating and drinking. He lends a willing ear to his counsellors, and decides nothing without asking them ; but in great matters he acts on his own judgment, and, in my opinion, he generally comes to a right decision. I recognise him perfectly in the conclusion of the last peace, made against the wishes of the majority in the kingdom.

"When he was a minor he was instigated by those who held the government to do some dishonourable things. They favoured his love intrigues with their relations in order to keep him in their subjection. As soon as he came of age and understood his duties he gave up these intrigues. When I arrived he was keeping a lady with great state in a castle. He visited her from time to time. Afterwards he sent her to her father's house, who is a knight, and married her. He did the same with another lady, by whom he had a son. It may be about a year since he gave up—so at least it is be-lieved—his love-making, as well from fear of

God as from fear of scandal in this world, which is thought very much of here. I can say with truth that he esteems himself as much as if he were Lord of the world. He loves war so well that I fear, judging by the provocation he receives, the peace will not be of long duration. . . ."

It will be observed that, according to Ayala, if those are right who place the beginning of James's connection with Margaret Drummond at an early date, he had not, in spite of his devotion, been faithful to his love. Though it would appear from the report of the envoy that there were times when he sought to amend his life, he united with the attraction and gifts belonging to the Stewart race the weakness and immorality to which they were prone. The time from which Ayala dates the reformation in his habits corresponds to that when Margaret was installed—possibly after some sort of marriage ceremony—at Stirling. As a matter of fact, and in spite of fits of remorse, morality in him continued to remain divorced from religious sentiment; and infatuation for a woman was not without its influence on the final catastrophe. At this time, however, it would seem that Margaret Drummond, the uncrowned Queen, had established her right to undivided sway, and the Spaniard, expressing a fear lest his description of James might seem to denote partiality, repeated that his virtues were great and his faults worthy of mention few.

It is difficult to believe that the ambassador had been guiltless of a smile as he submitted to his sovereigns, with whose tortuous diplomatic methods he was well acquainted, the views entertained by James with regard to the sacredness of a King's word. At this very time it was believed, wrongly or rightly, by another Spanish envoy that the King was still under the impression that an Infanta was to be bestowed upon him in marriage. It may be that he was less successfully duped than was imagined, and that he himself was not averse to indulging matrimonial projects doomed to prove fruitless. Something of the kind Ayala may have divined. Such a king as the King of Scotland, he wrote, was harder to marry than to bring up.

To Ayala belonged the chief credit of conducting the peace negotiations with England to a successful conclusion—a pacification which it has been seen that he himself considered of a precarious nature. It was, in fact, liable at any moment to be endangered by the aggressions of irresponsible skirmishers on either side of the Border, whose misdeeds were laid to the account of the country to which they chanced to belong. Peace of any kind was nevertheless better than the recognised hostility lately prevailing, and it says much for the tact and discretion of the foreign envoy, and the confidence he had succeeded in inspiring, that he was named by James sole commissioner on his behalf during the negotiations resulting in the preliminary truce of Aytoun. That the task set him was no easy one may be inferred from the report he sent to his government— true to his character of James's partisan— of certain occurrences threatening to render his labours vain.

"It is a wonder," he wrote, "that the peace is not already broken. The King of Scots has borne the injustice committed by the English only because the peace has been made by Spain." De Puebla also, Ayala's rival at the English court, acquitted James of any desire to infringe the conditions of the truce. "The King of Scots," he wrote, "'has seen the ears of the wolf,' and is now endeavouring 'to make a bed of roses' for the King of England. Two

9

or three months ago the English killed a great
number of Scots, but King James would not
permit the Scots to kill an equal number of
English. He only wrote a letter to Henry,
full of compliments and courtesy, as though he
had been a son writing to his father."

What had happened had been that a
party of Scots had visited Norham Castle, as
it would seem in a mere spirit of curiosity.
Though armed—as was no doubt necessary for
tourists of the day—they did no more than look
at the building with intelligent interest—they
" beheld it wondrous circumspectly, as though
they had been desirous to know what was done
there within." On this first occasion they
were permitted to withdraw, no question put.
When, however, they reappeared on the following day, some mischief was apprehended; they
were asked what their visit signified, " and
why they viewed and advised so the castle " ;
and when the Scots answered proudly, making
" blustering and blowing " replies, they were
given in return hard and manly strokes, and
some being slain and others wounded, the remainder rode off as rapidly as their horses could
carry them. When the matter was reported to
the King, he was sore moved, and swore by

sweet St. Ninian—a favourite saint of his—that
nothing was more inconstant and unsteadfast
than Henry's observance of the truce.

After all, no great harm came of the incident.
Henry desired nothing more than peace, and
answered James's complaints by disowning the
proceedings of the guardians of Norham Castle,
promising to visit any misdemeanour of which
they had been guilty with condign punishment.
The Bishop of Durham was once more chosen
as a messenger of peace ; and after conciliatory
letters had passed between him and James,
he received a communication from the King,
couched in terms of some mystery, inviting him
to an interview, when he would find his labour
well bestowed.

The meeting took place at Melrose, some
time in the year 1499 ; when the Bishop was
treated by James "with all humanity that
could be thought of." Face to face, alone
with the churchman, the King explained his
desire that the friendship—of recent date—existing between himself and Henry should be
confirmed and cemented by his marriage with
the Lady Margaret ; adding that so soon as he
should know the Bishop's mind on the subject
he would be ready to send ambassadors to

England to make the proposal in due form. The Bishop, as in duty bound, listened as if to a project freshly evolved. Since Henry had thrown out the same suggestion at intervals for some years, he can have felt little doubt as to his master's wishes, but his answer was made with dignified reserve, and he did no more than promise to use his endeavours to further the scheme.

It was not a day when matters of the kind were concluded with speed, and proceedings lagged. Nevertheless, in 1500, the papal dispensation was sought—bride and bridegroom being within the prohibited degrees ; and the marriage might be considered as within measurable distance. James had yielded, and had at length subscribed to the doctrine that kings are not free to dispose of themselves.

What Margaret Drummond thought of it, at Stirling with her baby daughter, we have no means of knowing. She was, after all, to be spared the pain of seeing her lover married to another woman. Whether or not the reported clandestine marriage had taken place— which is not likely—not long after the blow had fallen and James had given his promise to her supplanter, death stepped in to remove her from the scene. The exact date of the tragedy is not known, and it would seem, by an entry in the Treasurer's books, that she was still alive in 1502; but about that time it is certain that Margaret, her sister Lady Fleming, and another sister, Lady Sybilla Drummond, all three died suddenly, as it was believed, from poison.

The motives prompting the murder can only be conjectured. By some it was thought that jealousy of the house of Drummond, and the fear that the King would in truth make Margaret Queen, had caused it, her sisters having merely been involved in her misfortune; others have seen in the affair a simple domestic catastrophe. Be that as it may, Margaret Drummond was to prove no stumbling-block in the way of her English namesake; nor was James to be torn between fidelity to the past and loyalty to present pledges.

Margaret Drummond was not forgotten. In the church at Dunblane where she and her two young sisters lay, under the blue marble flags marking their resting-place, masses were regularly said for the repose of her soul until James's own death; and her little daughter was brought in 1503 from Drummond Castle to Stirling, to be reared as " the King's dochter " at court.

Thus the woman James had loved so well passed out of his life, and left him free to contract fresh ties without remorse.

CHAPTER IX

1500—1502

Work accomplished by James—His relations with his subjects—His popularity—His reforms—Ecclesiastical scandals—Negotiations for the English marriage—Marriage
treaty concluded—Death of Margaret's mother.

IT is worth pausing, in the story of his life,
to form some estimate of the work James IV
had achieved since his accession, or rather
during the years that had passed since he had
been of an age to assume the reins of government. Only by contrasting the condition of
the kingdom at the time of his father's death
with the law and order established in it before
the close of his own reign, is it possible to arrive
at a just view of the influence that a King—still
in his first youth—had succeeded in gaining
over the inhabitants of a realm he had found
in a state of disorder and tumult, class opposed
to class, clan to clan, internecine warfare ever
ready to break out, and the authority of the

Crown practically powerless to restrain the turbulence of the people.

Before James had reigned, even nominally, for ten years, all was transformed. There might be districts, such as the Western Islands, where rebellion, smouldering or open, continued unsuppressed, and the supremacy of law had not been vindicated; but over the whole face of the country a change had passed. Order had been called out of what had come near to being chaos. And this had been mainly accomplished by a King not yet twenty-five, and by the hold he had obtained over all classes of his subjects.

It is difficult in these days to realise the personal connection once existing between a sovereign and those who owed him allegiance. In our own time a King is a necessary part of the machinery of government and, as such, may command the respect and adherence of lovers of the constitution. But the circle within which he is an object of genuine affection is constantly narrowing, and loyalty, as a passion swaying thought and act, may be said to have ended with the extinction of the Stewart race. Men may still be found who would die for their country, should the sacrifice be demanded of them ; to be ready to give their life for their King would seem to savour of the romance belonging to an age that is past.

The reason—one of the reasons—for the change is not far to seek. In most countries in these modern days, all men, whether rich or poor, are aware that so far as the private welfare of the individual is concerned, it is a matter of comparatively little moment who is seated on the throne. To the public mind a monarch who is brave and honest and right-minded will doubtless make a stronger appeal than one who displays the opposite qualities. Nevertheless, he is so remote from the mass of his people that it is their imagination which is chiefly affected by his virtues, and it is rare that anything more than a surface enthusiasm is excited on the subject.

Four hundred years ago it was a wholly different matter. In some sense all men felt a personal interest in their King. His folly might imperil their safety ; his valour was a national possession ; his gifts and his graces were matter of pride ; his strength or his weakness factors that might transform their destinies. To an immeasurably larger proportion of his people he was personally known ; and it is only necessary to recall some of the items included in the Treasurer's accounts about this time to understand in some degree the tie that existed between the sovereign—when the sovereign was such a one as James IV—and the units who made up the nation:

" To a poor bairn that took the King by the hand, 3s.

" By the King's command to a travelling man by the gait [road], 9s.

" When the King departed, to the boy that brake his leg and lay still there, to his expenses and to pay for his leeching, 22s.

" To ane tale-teller that tellit tales to the King, 9s."

And if King and people were brought daily into contact, the present occupant of the throne was specially well calculated to arrest attention and awaken affection and sympathy.

It is true that, the manifold reforms he had initiated and carried into effect notwithstanding, his character was in not a few respects the reverse of that of the statesman and some at least of his failings might have been expected to militate against the prosperity of the country he ruled. A lover of war, his " young ad-

venturousness " had again and again imperilled
the kingdom ; and his lavish and profuse extravagance could not but press heavily on
the national finances.   Yet even while men
may have blamed him, these very failings—
the rashness with which he would invite a
trial of strength, the foolhardihood befitting
an irresponsible knight-errant rather than the
head of a nation, and the splendour and
magnificence of his court, costly though it
was—lent to the figure of the young King a
glamour without which he might have failed,
in spite of more solid attributes, to dominate as
he did the popular imagination.   His horseman-
ship, his skill in fencing and shooting, the
physical training by which he had accustomed
himself to be indifferent to all kinds of weather
or to want of rest, his gallantry, his spirit of
adventure, his carelessness as to money—often
carried to exaggeration—all played their part
in rendering him a striking personality.   In
spite of the occasional disapproval of wiser or
cooler heads, he commanded to the end the
loyalty and love of his people, proud of their
King, of the renown he had won, not only at
home but abroad, and of the gifts that attracted
foreigners to his court.

To others who might have been alienated by his faults, he was commended by his deep religious feeling, dissociated as it was from moral restraint. "His piety," says Pinkerton plainly, "was as violent as his disposition to amorous sin"—a piety finding expression in the erection of monasteries and churches, in the fervency of his devotions, and the pilgrimages made to the shrines of his favourite saints, "sweet St. Ninian" and others. No doubt, too, the wearing of the iron girdle was a fact that affected those around him with pity and compassion for the remorse that had not ceased to darken his youth.

Whatever causes had contributed to give him the power he possessed, he used it mostly wisely, so far as domestic matters were concerned. By a well-timed severity he had contrived to put an end to the perpetual quarrels of the great nobles ; whilst his reputation for strict justice, combined with humanity, spreading through the country at large, conduced to curb the turbulence of the lower classes. Ayala, making his observations with the interest of a foreigner and the shrewdness of a keen observer of the country to which he had been sent, noted, with regard to the inhabitants of the wilder regions,

that James was "feared by the bad and loved
and revered by the good like a god." People
had been taught by experience that he executed
the law without respect to rich or poor. Yet if
severe he was also just, and according to
Drummond, "rather shook his sword than
struck with it." It was observed, too, as proof
of his self-control, that he never changed colour
in anger at any offence, nor for any news that
was brought him.[1]

"I am told," the Spaniard also reported,
"that Scotland has improved so much during
his reign that it is worth three times more
now than formerly, on account of foreigners
having come to the country and taught them
how to live. . . . There is as great a difference
between the Scotland of old time and the Scotland of to-day as there is between good and
bad." It was high praise.

An abuse he had found prevailing—the
farming out of the administration of justice—
was abolished, "because justice was not well
administered in that way." Nor was he content
to trust to the reports of subordinates ; his own
eye was over all, and in 1497 he presided in
person at the courts of law held in many of

[1] Drummond.

the Western Islands, still the most disturbed part of the country.

Through love and through fear he had established his supremacy in his kingdom. He was emphatically master. What he thought right he did, regardless of the opinions of others —as when, finally determining that war with England should cease, he concluded a peace in the teeth of the majority of his subjects, who were, according to Ayala, opposed to a pacification.

It was of course impossible that all the reforms to which he had set his hand could be carried into effect at once, and the recurrent disturbances in the west continued for some time longer, the struggle between the royal authority and the rebellious and lawless spirit of the island chieftains being attended with varying results. Not until 1503 and the two following years, did campaigns conducted against the insurgents on a large scale succeed in quelling their resistance. That defeat would seem to have been accepted without resentment may have been due in part to the fact that, so soon as peace with England left James leisure to attend to domestic affairs, he renewed his visits to the islands and gave his personal supervision to the steps taken to restore order. "It is a signal tribute to the justice of James's dealings," says Mr. Hume Brown, "that none of his subjects followed him more loyally to the field of Flodden than the men whose country had so often felt the force of his arm."

In matters ecclesiastical, in spite of his piety, he is less to be admired. He was in close relations with the Roman court, and it was probably through his influence that Glasgow, the traditional rival of St. Andrews, was raised to be an archiepiscopal see—a favour destined to prove unfortunate, since the emulation between the two archbishops rose to such a height that Parliament was forced to intervene with a threat that, should their quarrels not cease, their rents would be suspended. With regard to church patronage, Scotland was in a condition causing scandal wherever it was known, nor was James's conduct calculated to lessen it. In 1497 his brother, the Duke of Ross, was made, at twenty-one, Archbishop of St. Andrews ; and he was succeeded by the King's illegitimate son when still a minor. Another son was made Abbot of Dunfermline; three benefices were conferred upon James's secretary, and his treasurer was first promoted to the bishopric of Galloway and then made Archbishop of Glasgow.

It has been seen that the cessation of hostilities with England had in no sense left James free from occupation, and that his leisure was largely employed in quelling disturbances at home. But, even had the western districts given him less to do, time was, in no case, likely to hang heavy on his hands. Music, poetry, architecture—almost every form of art—claimed his attention. Should other interests and occupations fail, there were experiments to be tried, as when he caused a dumb woman with two infants to be sequestrated from human intercourse, in order that it might be seen what language the children would speak. "Some say," asserts Lindsay of Pitscottie, "they spake good Hebrew," adding honestly that he was ignorant on what authority this fact rested. To later years belonged James's attempts, by means of an Italian upon whom he conferred an abbey, to convert base metal into gold. The same abbot also undertook to fly by means of wings, and started from the castle wall at Stirling on his way to France. The flight proved a short one and the airman fell and broke his thigh bone, charging the blame for the disaster upon a fault in the manufacture of the wings. Hen feathers, he complained, had been put into them, thus accounting for their failure to sustain him.

In the meantime the negotiations concerning the English alliance were proceeding. In April 1501, the death of Henry VII's elder son had brought Margaret one step nearer in succession to the throne and had proportionately heightened her value in the estimation of the Scottish Council. In the October of that year three plenipotentiaries were appointed to proceed to England to make final arrangements for the marriage. These were the Archbishop of Glasgow, Patrick Hepburn, Earl of Bothwell, and Andrew Forman, Bishop of Moray, now beginning to play a conspicuous part in European diplomacy, and unusually successful, not only in retaining the confidence of his master, but in propitiating, to his personal advantage, all the powers to whom he was in turn accredited. His former post of pronotary to Alexander VI was a position not conducive to the high reputation of the man who had held it ; and the preferments bestowed on him abroad are justly considered to throw doubts upon his

10

trustworthiness as an agent. The Abbey of Cottingham, presented to him by Henry VII on the conclusion of his daughter's marriage treaty, would not have been given for nothing. It has been conjectured that it was in recognition of some abatement of the dower to be brought to James by his bride that the gift was made.

It was when the marriage was under discussion that the scene at the English Council Board so often quoted took place. Margaret being next heir to her brother, England, it was objected, might chance to become a province of Scotland.

" No," replied Henry, " the smaller will ever follow the larger kingdom."

The match was approved by most people on either side of the Tweed. One person was strong in his dissent from the opinion of the majority ; and when the little Prince Henry was bidden to salute his sister as James's betrothed, his passionate indignation took all present by surprise, the ague from which he subsequently suffered being attributed by one writer to the effect of his anger and fury.

The boy's wrath notwithstanding, the matter was finally concluded on January 24th, 1502 ;

HENRY VII.
From a painting by Jan de Mabuse.

with the signature of two other treaties besides
the marriage contract.

According to this " Indenture for Peace and
Friendship," there was to be " a good, real,
sincere, true, sound, and firm peace, friendship,
league and confederation, to last to all time
coming," between the Kings of Scotland and
England, their kingdoms and subjects. Neither
James nor Henry nor their successors were to
make war, or cause war to be made against the
other and his heirs, nor give aid, either openly
or secretly, for the urging on of war. Rebels
and traitors were not to be harboured, but to
be imprisoned and handed over, if required,
within twenty days. Should either prince be
attacked by any other, of whatever dignity,
that prince whose realm had not been attacked
was to assist the other with such forces as were
requested, and with all speed, and should be
paid for the same, nor was any former treaty
to be considered an obstacle to the present
arrangement. Berwick was to remain in English hands, and the King of Scots and his vassals
were not to be attacked by English subjects
belonging to Berwick. A list of the allies on
either side followed, with permission to each
King to give aid to his ally, " but not by an in-

vasion of the other's territory." The sanction of the Pope to this treaty was to be obtained, and he who broke it was to be excommunicated.[1]

Thus was perpetual peace between the ancient enemies sworn, no loophole of escape being permitted from the terms of the engagement. It may be questioned whether either of the parties were the dupes of their own promises.

With regard to the marriage itself, Henry, as was his thrifty custom, had made a good bargain so far as financial arrangements were concerned. James was to pay his wife a yearly income equal to £6,000, the sum of £10,000 sterling comprising the whole of the dowry she brought. After this, it is somewhat singular to find Henry VIII, in 1536, in reply to one of his sister's constant demands for money, expressing his surprise by reason of the liberality with which their father had provided for her on her marriage.

On the day following the signing of the three compacts the marriage ceremony was performed, Bothwell acting as James's proxy. The affair was of a quieter nature than might have been expected, owing to the delicate health of the bride's mother. The service took place

---

[1] *Days of James IV*, Gregory Smith, from Rymer.

in the Queen's apartments at Richmond Palace, a curious feature of it being the presence of Lady Katharine Gordon, wife of Perkin War-beck, who by right of her blood connection with both bride and bridegroom took rank next to the royal family itself.

The usual questions were asked and answered ; the troth was plighted ; the royal trumpeters blew their trumpets ; minstrels responded in joyful guise. Margaret had become a Queen, to be treated and honoured as such. Hand in hand with her mother, as equal with equal, she moved to the room where the wedding banquet was spread, to be succeeded by a tournament at which the prizes were bestowed upon the victors by the bride.

More than eighteen months were to elapse before Margaret was transferred to her husband's keeping ; but James was no longer a free man. The seal had been set, at long last, upon the often meditated matrimonial alliance between England and Scotland.

What her mother thought of an arrangement by which her little daughter was to be delivered over to a bridegroom more than double her age, and unknown to her and her parents even by sight, can only be conjectured. As it proved,

Elizabeth was to be spared the pain of seeing her child sent to a foreign land. On February 11th, 1503, a little more than a year after the marriage ceremony, she died. To the anticipated grief of a parting which was not to take place, Sir Thomas More refers in the elegy he wrote upon the occasion of the Queen's death:

> Farewell, my daughter, Lady Margaret,
> God wot full oft it grievèd hath my mind,
> That ye should go where we should seldom meet;
> Now I am gone and have left you behind.
> Oh mortal folk that we be very blind,
> What we least fear, full oft it is most nigh,
> From you depart I first, and lo, now here I lie."

CHAPTER X

1503

Margaret comes to Scotland—Her journey and meeting with James—The marriage ceremony—Her letter to her father.

IT was August 1503 when Margaret Tudor was brought to her new home, some weeks before the date stipulated in the marriage contract; and the interval between her departure from her father's court and the inauguration of her future life at Edinburgh stands out clearly portrayed in the narrative of the Somerset Herald, John Young, who was a member of her train. Every incident of her journey, the honours paid her, the pageants attending her progress, are all related in elaborate detail; so that it is possible for those who care to do so to assist at her reception in the English towns through which she passed in her double character of Princess of England and Queen of Scotland, to watch her crossing, in peace and amity, the border-land where so much blood had been shed in the course of the age-long feud her coming was intended to heal ; and—of greater interest— to be present at her meeting with James.

All this is told, not an incident omitted. The inner history of those weeks is a different matter ; nor is there anything save the pitiful letter of a homesick child, when, the momentous journey accomplished, she was to be left in Scottish hands, to show whether, the first novelty of her triumphal progress over, and satiated with ceremonies and pomps, the heart of the little central figure of the show had failed her at the thought that the familiar surroundings of her childhood were left behind her for ever, and that, with the exception of the few attendants and officials who were to share her exile, strangers and foreigners were alone to be her associates and companions.

Neither is there anything, except the tone of pettish complaint discernible in the same letter, to tell what was the impression made upon her by the man to whose care she was to be entrusted ; nor any evidence to show what James thought of the girl—she was not fourteen— whom he had consented to accept as his wife. With all the Tudor characteristics latent in her —their caprice, self-will, passion, and selfish-

ness—she can have seemed to him at present
little more than a child—and possibly an un-
attractive one—whom he had been compelled,
by the exigencies of politics and statecraft, to
place in the position he had desired to bestow
upon the other Margaret he had loved.

On July 8th the parting—it was to be a final
one—between Henry and his daughter had
taken place at Coleweston, where he had
brought her to take leave of his mother. It
had been settled beforehand—not unwisely,
in dealing with a man as much addicted to
economy as the first of the Tudors—that Henry
should be responsible for the cost of the
Queen's journey, until the boundary of his
kingdom had been reached ; and for once he
appears to have recognised the necessity of a
lavish outlay. The Earl of Surrey—always
destined to cross James's path, whether in peace
or war—was chief in command of the bride's
escort ; and as one stage after another of the
progress was reached her train was constantly
swelled by bishops, nobles, gentlemen and great
ladies, who gave up their places in turn to others,
as the particular locality to which they belonged
was left behind.

Towns, districts, nobles and civic officials

vied with each other in doing honour to the daughter of their sovereign and the messenger of peace ; and at every step ceremonial observances were arranged to welcome her, with pageants and shows of all kinds.

The journey, under these circumstances, took time, and it was not until July 30th that Berwick was reached. Two days later, the Queen had crossed the Border, arriving with a great company magnificently arrayed at Lambertonkirk, where she was received on King James's behalf by the Archbishop of Glasgow and the Earl of Morton, also splendidly attended. "And there were five trumpets or clarions of the said King that blew at the coming of the said Queen. The which melody was good to hear and see."

At Dalkeith the meeting with James himself took place. There he first saw the girl who was to be the companion of the last ten years of his life, and the mother of his heir. There is little to enable us to call up a picture of Margaret at this date. At the time that Mabuse painted her and her two brothers she can scarcely have been more than three or four years old, and the small hooded head with its broad marked brows and delicate features is not without a childish charm—a charm wholly lacking in the portraits of the older woman. In youth she had probably the Tudor fairness of skin, and her hair was golden. Further details there are none, and the panegyrics of her beauty contained in the verses of Dunbar, in his character of court poet, do not carry conviction. In any case, James was not a man to whom the immature graces of a child of thirteen would appeal. But whatever may have been his private sentiments, the gentle consideration, the chivalrous deference, and the courtesy shown by the King towards his little bride during the days following upon her arrival in his kingdom can have left nothing to be desired even in the jealous eyes of her English attendants.

Half a mile from Dalkeith a halt had been made, in order that she might be attired yet more richly. On her entrance to the castle she was received by the Earl of Morton as its lady and mistress, and was presented with the keys ; whilst Lady Morton awaited her on her knees. "The said Queen took her up and kissed her, and so she was conveyed to her chamber. . . ."

Though no formal meeting with the King had been as yet arranged, impatient of preliminaries, he had come to hawk in the neighbourhood, and now made his unexpected appearance at the castle, wearing a crimson velvet jacket, his lure slung over his shoulder, his beard somewhat long; and with it all, as Don Pedro de Ayala had said, as handsome as a man could be. In spite of his thirty years he was a bridegroom of whom Margaret might well have been proud.

He was attended by his brother, the Archbishop of St. Andrews, and by a crowd of nobles, and was forthwith conducted to the Queen's apartment, " where she met him at her great chamber door right honourably accompanied. At the meeting he and she made great reverences the one to the other, his head being bare, and they kissed together, and in like wise kissed the ladies and others also, and he in especial welcomed the Earl of Surrey right heartily. Then the Queen and he went aside and communed together by long space. . . ."

Supper followed, with much ceremonial; minstrels played; and when the meal was over, Margaret, with Lady Surrey, danced before the court. "This done, the King took leave of her, for it was late, and he went to his bed at Edinburgh, very well content "—as the Somerset Herald boldly assumed—" of so fair meeting."

That very night was marked by a mishap,
a fire breaking out at the stables, when
Margaret's two white palfreys were burnt. In
the afternoon of the following day James paid
a second visit to the castle, " coming for to see
the Queen again and to comfort her " for her
loss. His arrival being on this occasion anticipated, a great company, including an English
and a Scottish archbishop, Surrey, and Bothwell, had gone to meet him. Avoiding the
formality of a reception and—once more according to the Herald—" flying as a bird that
seeks his prey," he took another road, and
coming privily to the castle, entered the Queen's
chamber with no more than a few companions
and found her playing at cards, " who received
him very gladly and of good will kissing him."

Dancing again followed, and when that was
over, James contributed to the entertainment of
the company by playing on the lute and the
clavichord. Sir Edward Stanley, too, sang a
ballad, winning great commendation from the
King. Calling for a gentleman of his own,
also a musician, James made the two sing together, " the which accorded very well." . . .
" After all these things fulfilled, the King took
license of the Queen and kissed her . . . and went

to his horse, on whom he did leap without putting the foot within the stirrup ; and the said horse was right fair courser, and incontinent the King spurred, follow who might."

Finding that he had been pursued by Surrey and many other knights and nobles, he presently turned with his accustomed courtesy and, bareheaded, met the English earl, riding with him some little way before parting for the night.

So the days passed by, the delay that intervened before the actual marriage being possibly intended to afford time for bride and bridegroom to become to some degree acquainted. It may be that James found his part easier to play in connection with so mere a child than would have been the case had Margaret been a woman, and a woman to whom he had no heart to give. At any rate, all went well.

Again and again little touches in the narrative of the chronicler—much concerned with pomps and ceremonies and with the magnificent apparel of the persons concerned in them—call up the picture of the pair. Now they are drawing apart from the crowd of courtiers to a spot where unfortunately John Young cannot follow them, that they may hold private converse.

Another time, kneeling bareheaded at Margaret's side, the King plays to her on the lute. Or again, as the two sit at supper together, he observes that her stool is not " for her comfort " and insists upon vacating his own chair in her favour. Palfreys were given her in compensation for those burnt at Dalkeith, and all was done that could be devised to conduce to her amusement and pleasure.

On August 7th a start was made towards Edinburgh. Dressed in a magnificent garment of cloth of gold, Margaret was carried in a litter, to be met on her way by a great tame hart, sent by James, in order that her journey might be enlivened by the chase. Surrey having, however, decreed that the hunt was not to take place until the King himself could share in it, the procession moved on till half-way between Dalkeith and Edinburgh James appeared, riding a bay, and galloping to meet his bride. Leaping from his horse, he kissed her as she sat in her litter, before, mounting again, he turned to accompany her to the capital, where a fresh arrangement was made and the two rode together on the same palfrey through the town, so that all citizens might see their new Queen.

It is not necessary to linger over the functions which attended her entry. Joy-bells rang ; the town was hung with tapestries ; everywhere shows and pageants met the royal train. The church of St. Cross was visited, a Te Deum was sung, and a great reception followed at the palace, whither James, bareheaded and with his arm about her, had led the Queen. With the Bishop of Moray—always a prominent figure— at hand to present each lady to her in turn, Margaret went from guest to guest, and " after she had kissed them all, the King kissed her for her labour," brought her back to her chamber and took his leave right humbly, before he went to seek his lodging and the long day's work was at length over.

The next morning—it was August 8th—the marriage was celebrated with all due magnifi- cence and the ill-matched couple—James, a man in the prime of life, and with years of experience behind him, and Margaret, a child " with her hair hanging "—were made man and wife. At her side her *gouvernante* had been ready to prompt her charge where such prompt- ing was necessary, the anointing of the Queen followed upon the marriage ceremony, and James placed the sceptre in her hand. All

JAMES IV, KING OF SCOTLAND.
From an old Dutch print.

had been done, and the evening ended with a great banquet, dancing and merry-making.

The succeeding days were crowded with every species of entertainment, jousts, games, tournaments. In one of the sham fights James, disguised as the " savage knight," took part, at the head of a body of rough highlanders and borderers who declined to confine themselves to mere harmless fencing. That blood was shed was, in the opinion of the chronicler, of little importance, considering who were the victims. King Arthur and his knights were also represented in the lists, and Dunbar, the court poet, composed in honour of the occasion his verses on " The Thistle and the Rose." Dunbar was a courtier, but with a poet's licence he proceeded—after a panegyric upon James, as " the Lion, greatest of degree "—to represent Dame Nature as addressing a not unneeded admonition to " the awful Thistle " to deal worthily with " the fresh rose, of colour red and white " entrusted to his care :

And sen thow art a King, thow be discreit ;
Herb without vertew thow hald nocht of sic pryce,
As herb of vertew and of odor sueit,
And lat no nettill vyle and full of vyce
Hir fallow to the gudly flour delyce,
Nor lat no wyld weid full of churlicheness
Compair hir till the lilleis nobilness.

II

The poem ended with praise of the rose of most delight, queen and sovereign of all other flowers.

In this manner was Margaret Tudor welcomed to Scotland. It might have been imagined that she would have been well pleased with the prospect opening out before her, that the new-made Queen had been dazzled by the bridegroom she had found awaiting her, gallant and courteous, and that her heart had been won by his gentle consideration and the kindness he had displayed. On the other hand, it may be that, homesick and desolate, she was in no mood to be touched by his grace and attraction, and was tempted to charge upon him, however unjustly, the responsibility for the fact that she had been sent, a stranger, to a foreign land and separated from all that she had loved; that she regarded herself as a victim to political expediency and owed him a grudge in consequence.

This might be the inference drawn from the letter sent to her father by the hands of those of her train who were returning to England, and from its tone of fretful discontent.

Commending all her servants to Henry, she

begs him to give credence to the lady who was
to be the bearer of her letter, " for I have showed
her more of my mind than I will write at this
time." Nothing was said of her splendid reception, nothing of the King and his welcome ;
there was no news to send her father, so she
wrote, save that my Lord of Surrey was in
such favour with the King that he could not
forgo his company at any time of the day.
Surrey and the Bishop of Moray were ordering
all things as nearly as they could to James's
pleasure ; " I pray God it may be for my poor
heart's ease in time to come." Her chamberlain
was not called to take counsel with them, though
better fitted than any to do so. If he spoke
on her behalf, Surrey answered in such wise
that he dared say no more. " God send me
comfort to His pleasure, and that I and mine
who be left here with me be well entreated, such
ways as they have taken." So far the letter
had been dictated ; but now Margaret takes the
pen into her own hand. " For God's sake, Sir,
hold me excused that I write not myself to your
Grace, for I have no leisure this time, but with
a wish I would I were with your Grace now
and many times more, when I would answer.
As for this that I have written to your Grace,

it is very true, but I pray God I may find it well for my welfare hereafter. . . ."

Thus the letter of the lonely child ends ; and after this fashion was inaugurated the marriage destined to produce results so momentous in the history of both England and Scotland.

CHAPTER XI

1503—1508

Margaret as Queen—James's Court—Death of a child of
the King—Janet Kennedy—Death of the Duke of
Ross—James rebukes the Duke of Gueldres—Afterwards
protects him—Assists Denmark—Honoured by the Pope.

I⊤ would have been interesting to learn how
the country to which she had been brought
compared with her own in the critical eyes of
the English bride. If Ayala's account is to be
trusted, it should have struck her not unfavour-
ably. Treating of Scottish women in particular, he noted their extreme courtesy and, in
spite of their boldness, their honesty. Before
their time in this respect, they were absolute
mistresses in their houses ; even their husbands
submitted to their authority, and it was by the
wives that the family property was administered
and the expenditure ruled. Graceful and handsome, they dressed, in the foreigner's opinion,
far better than the English ladies. The houses

were comfortable, provided with doors and glass windows, and were well furnished.

Such was the outward aspect of Margaret's new surroundings. Her life promised to be a gay one, and when her English escort took their way home the accounts they will have given Henry of James and his court must have convinced him that his daughter was not likely to suffer from dulness. The ease and familiarity of the relations established between the King and his wife's countrywomen is evidenced by entries in the Treasurer's accounts recording the rich rewards bestowed upon Lady Surrey and her daughter, Lady Gray, for having " clipped the King's beard."

Now her old friends were gone, save those that were to remain, like their mistress, in honourable banishment, and she was left to find her own way in her new life. The picture of the court over which she was to preside as Queen has been sketched by the various chroniclers, each adding his touch of colour to the scene, with its gaiety, its manifold amusements, its thronging guests, native and foreign. The principal figure, notwithstanding his thirty years, is still something of a Prince Charming, though possessing more virile attributes than are commonly associated with that character of fairy tale and romance. Courteous and easy of access, endowed with beauty and attraction, full of manifold interests, all of kindred tastes flock around him as to their natural centre, whilst yet there is no trace of any man having occupied at his court the place of favourite. Even the rough nobles who had slain his father and to whom submission to authority of whatever kind was no habit or tradition, have laid down their arms and accepted as their master the man they had carried away from Stirling fifteen years earlier as the figurehead of their rebellion, and whom they had doubtless expected to make their instrument and tool. To the reputation he had won, not only at home but abroad, Erasmus's description bears witness : " He had a wonderful force of intellect, an astounding knowledge of everything, an invincible magnanimity, the dignity of a true King, the greatest courtesy, and the most abounding liberality."

Beside this brilliant personality stands the little Queen, looking longingly back at her lost home and the father she had left, " with a wish I would I were with your Grace." The contrast is sharp, and the forlornness of the bride evokes compassion. It may be that James, with his quick and sympathetic intelligence, divined something at least of her condition of mind. He would seem to have done what he could, when her English associates had departed, to replace them and to reconcile the stranger to her unfamiliar environment. His evenings were spent playing cards with her; he made her rich and costly gifts, and filled her days with amusement. And all this though, not more than a month after his wedding day, the festivities had been interrupted, so far as he himself was concerned, by a blow that, though it was one to be borne in silence, must have hit him hard. The laconic entries in the Treasurer's accounts alone remain to tell how one of his children—and James loved his children well—had passed away at Stirling:

"For a horse to ride to Edinburgh to warn the King of the dying of one of the bairns, 5s.

"For a winding sheet for the said bairn, 2s."

No other record is to be found of the private grief that followed so hard upon the public rejoicing. "One of the bairns." There is nothing to tell who was the dead child's mother; but it is curious to think of the arrival of the

messenger with his tidings of misfortune, to be
heedfully kept from the ears of the new-made
wife, and of the shadow cast for James upon the
merry-making.

For a time it might be possible to keep
Margaret in ignorance of much in the past that
augured ill for the future. It would not be
possible for long. For the misgivings visible in
her letter to her father there was more foundation than she was, at the time it was written,
aware of; and she cannot long have remained
unacquainted with facts that must have been
well known to every member of her husband's
court. It was true that Margaret Drummond
was dead, and the menace she would have
embodied removed; but Janet Kennedy,
daughter of Lord Kennedy and sometimes
called Lady Bothwell,[1] lived—a woman who
had been Margaret's rival, and in some sort
had replaced her in the King's affections.
Whether or no, as some say, Janet had been the
mistress of the old Earl of Angus, or his betrothed
wife, as others believe, he had been supplanted
by his master, and in 1499 Janet had become
the mother of a son to whom James gave
his own name. Upon Janet herself he be-

----

[1] This title seems very variously bestowed.

stowed, two years later, the castle and estate
of Dernaway, in Elgin, where he was accustomed to hunt, though prudently making the
gift conditional upon her fidelity—" so long as
she shall remain without husband or other man,
with the King and his well-beloved son, James
Stewart." The death of Margaret Drummond
has been sometimes ascribed to the jealousy
of the Kennedy family, but though this is not
unlikely, there is no proof of it. At the date
of James's marriage he appears to have severed
for a time all other connections; it was
scarcely possible, however, that a man of his
nature and antecedents should remain faithful
to a child of fourteen, nor was it long before
old habits resumed their sway.

How soon Margaret became aware of the
state of things there is no evidence to show.
Tale-bearers will not have been wanting to en-
lighten her, nor was it a time when the ignorance belonging to childhood was prolonged.

For the present all went well. Before many
weeks had gone by the entertainments provided at Edinburgh were varied by a series
of visits paid to the towns and palaces of her
adopted country, ending with the castle of
Stirling, whence James had gone forth, fifteen

years earlier, to take the field against his father and had gained a crown and a burden of life-long remorse.

Christmas was passed at Edinburgh, when a certain Master John, a French leech, was master of the revels ; costly gems were pre-sented to the Queen, and James's lavish gener-osity was apparent in the gifts he made to her attendants.

Again death came to interrupt the festivities. The New Year was hardly begun before James's young brother, the Duke of Ross, Archbishop of St. Andrews, suddenly died, to the great sorrow of the King, who loved him much.

Parliament met in March, and Margaret's coronation took place ; her dower was confirmed, and the domain and castle of Kilmarnock was further conferred upon her. Henry VII had every reason to be satisfied, from a pecuniary point of view, and made his acknowledgment of the honourable manner in which James had carried out the marriage treaty.

In other respects James's value as a friend and ally of England was to be promptly demonstrated. When his cousin, the Duke of Gueldres, rendered himself troublesome by affording harbourage and countenance to the

English malcontent, Edmund de la Pole, representing the claims of the House of York, the
King of Scots was quick to interpose on behalf
of his father-in-law, and to call the Duke to
account.

His letter to the culprit contained an indignant rebuke, and was that of an angry man
who was taking no pains to measure his language.

" It is useless to excuse yourself to men of
experience with a feigned pretext of mediation,"
he wrote. " You make but a lame defence of
your innocence. Nothing could justify you in
departing from your promise for the sake of a
perfidious man without consulting me, to whom
you had bound yourself." It was a thing
certain and sure that Henry would now listen
to no composition. No prince was in the habit
of making peace with a subject. A King was
merciful to a subject when he was worthy of
forgiveness. James would fain believe that
Pole had come to Gueldres without licence
from the Duke. As to the refugee's talk of
armed men, it was an absurdity to pretend that
a needy person, supplied by the Duke with food,
could maintain a thousand soldiers under arms
and in his pay. " I wish you had refrained

from empty threats and from talking of his
boasted power. . . . Excuse me, illustrious
cousin, if I deal not gently with you now.
You treat with kindness a rebel of England,
an exile from the greater part of Christendom,
to the disgust of your friends and to the com-
plication even of your own affairs. . . . Is this
what has come of our supplications ? . . . Have
your promises come to this ? Over trustful
that I was, I represented you to my most
illustrious father, the King of England, as a
well-meaning and friendly prince : you openly
declare yourself his enemy, and the sole refuge
of his rebels." And the letter ends with
adjurations to the Duke to get quickly rid of
his " hateful guest."

The curious thing is that whilst the Duke
was upbraided and taken to task for his kindness to Pole, the fact was that, on whatever
terms he had been first received in Gueldres,
the refugee was kept there in confinement,
and was sending urgent entreaties to Philip
of Castile " to get him out of the hands of that
man." In the course of the year 1505 he was
dismissed from the duchy, and any intention
that the Duke may have entertained of making
capital out of his pretensions was abandoned.

On the other hand, when, four years later, the Duke was menaced by a hostile combination composed of Philip of Castile, Maximilian, King of the Romans, and Henry, James was no less firm in his cousin's defence than he had formerly been severe in his condemnation. In spite of the possibility that his attitude might involve trouble with England, he was in no way disposed to see his kinsman wronged or to shrink from adopting the cause of the weaker party in a dispute. Writing to his father-in-law in terms as uncompromising as those he had used to the Duke, he warned him plainly of the consequences, so far as he himself was concerned, should Henry join forces with the Duke's antagonists :

" If you, unmindful of any ties of blood, affinity, and alliance with him, should endeavour to prostrate my cousin, the Duke of Gueldres, or should take up arms against him, and, contrary to law and justice, should expel him from his paternal seat, I, who believe that in war justice will prevail over wrong, shall be sorrowfully compelled to esteem you as an enemy ; and shall be constrained to oppose your troops, and for the sake of justice and necessity to repel force. . . ."

The death of Philip of Castile put an end
to the quarrel for the present, and James was
not forced to take up arms against his " most
illustrious father." But the episode demonstrated the precarious nature of a peace which
had been called eternal.

Scotland, under a sovereign loved and
honoured at home, was learning to render itself
of no small account in the affairs of Europe.
The attention bestowed by James on naval
matters was calculated to increase his influence abroad. An alliance with his uncle
the King of Denmark, made in the earlier years
of his reign, had bound each to mutual defence,
and in 1502 James was called upon, in fulfilment of the compact, to send ships and men
to the assistance of King John in his quarrel
with Sweden. In 1506 he was again intervening
for the protection of his ally, and a letter of
that year to Queen Christina congratulates her
on the heroism with which she had endured a
six months' siege, and upon the conclusion of
the war. " That long siege had moved us
deeply," James wrote, " . . . wherefore we sent
a fleet of our subjects to Copenhagen, who,
having the less to do, have returned to us more
speedily than expected. We should in no wise

have tolerated this, nor would they have ever dared to do so, unless they had brought back word that you were safe, and that no danger threatened you. . . . To whom will I be a friend if not to you and yours ? . . ."

James was indeed a good friend. Faithfulness to pledges, rash though they might have been, was mainly the cause of the final catastrophe, and again and again he is found using his power for the protection of his neighbours. The needs of Denmark were not at an end ; and though he did his best to compose her quarrel with Lübeck during the following years he ended by dispatching Robert Barton and Andrew Wood, the best sailors Scotland had at her command, to supplement the Danish forces.

With Rome he was on the best of terms until close upon the end of his reign, notwithstanding the scandals in the way of ecclesiastical preferment countenanced by him or in which he was personally concerned ; and in 1507 he was presented by Pope Julius II with a purple hat and a sword with a golden scabbard, together with the title of " Protector of the Christian Religion." This mark of favour was said to be bestowed on the ground that James was the only prince considered by the Pope to be inclined towards peace—a singular tribute to be paid by a pontiff himself so bellicose.

At home all went well, and the kingdom prospered. The Parliament which met during the spring following upon the King's marriage had been noteworthy in many respects. Efforts were made to settle the affairs of the Highlands and Western Islands, at length definitely reduced to submission ; statutes were passed dealing with the better administration of justice ; burghs and merchants were confirmed in the possession of the ancient privileges " granted by our sovereign Lord's progenitors, of most noble mind." The letting of lands, whether royal or other, was facilitated, with a view to the improvement of the country, and the vassal was exempted from military service. Lastly, the King revoked all grants, gifts, Acts of Parliament or of general councils prejudicial to the Catholic Church, to his soul, or to his crown—a comprehensive measure of which it would be difficult to fix the limits.

The new friendliness with England was well maintained, and when James headed an expedition for the purpose of dislodging a certain gang of freebooters from the fastnesses of

12

Eskdale, Lord Dacre, English Warden on the Border, supplied the Scottish forces with presents of venison and other provisions. As usual the King triumphed. Some of the culprits were summarily executed, others were reserved for trial at Dumfries, and quiet was restored to the disturbed district. At this time indeed the kingdom was reduced to a condition of order and tranquillity so great that, according to Bishop Lesley, the King was able to take a solitary ride from Stirling to Perth and from Aberdeen to Elgin, where he rested " on a hard bed " at the house of one Thomas Leslie, a parson, reaching St. Duthac's in Ross in time to assist at Mass the next morning. It was a signal tribute to the success of his administration.

CHAPTER XII

1503—1508

Private life—Expeditions and journeys—Generosity to the
Queen—Her causes of discontent—James's varying moods
—Retreats and pilgrimages—Birth and death of a
Prince—James intends to visit the Holy Land.

SUCH was the history of the King, his interests,
occupations, and successes, during the years
following upon his marriage. In 1508 the tide
of prosperity consequent upon the firmness of
his rule and the peace, foreign and domestic,
that he had established, reached its height.
Not more than thirty-five, he might well be
content with what he had achieved, and have
looked forward to watching for many years the
development of the results of his labours.

Side by side with the record of his public life,
runs that, less complete and less creditable, of
his private one—the history of the man.

His endeavours to render his wife happy
appear to have been carried on for some time.
His court continued to be, what it had ever

been, a place of gaiety and pleasure ; James too was constantly on the move, and Margaret, not seldom the companion of his journeys, can have had no cause to complain of monotony. Expeditions were made, sometimes to the more remote districts of the country, at other times to spots nearer home. Thus we read of a summer excursion to the island of May, in the Firth of Forth, when, according to James's wont, he combined religious observance with pleasure, and Margaret was deputed to visit the small chapel on the island and to make an offering to the priest ; whilst the King paid his respects to the hermit who had chosen this solitary spot for his habitation. The ship which had conveyed the royal party to May afforded them lodging by night, and by day the King rowed over to the mainland, leaving Margaret to explore the island.

On other occasions, journeys were made by road in homely fashion, and the Queen, when thirsty, would call at a cottage and ask to drink.

In the matter of money James had treated his wife with generosity, and had increased the sum agreed upon as her dower in the marriage treaty—an act to which her father, not to be outdone, responded by sending a gift of 5,000 marks to defray the costs of his daughter's journey after the Border had been crossed. All therefore was outwardly prospering; yet the forebodings of trouble " for her poor heart " expressed in Margaret's first letter to her father must have been more than justified as time went on. If the King had determined when he brought home his bride to remain faithful to her, it was a resolution quickly broken, and it cannot have been long before Margaret was aware of it. Young though she was, she was a Tudor, with a Tudor's passions, a Tudor's jealousies; and in spite of the amusements her husband provided for her—the dances, the tournaments, the English minstrels and the like—the knowledge that she had been no more than a political necessity to the man she had married cannot have failed to rankle. No longer a child, to be reconciled to her lot by plays and pastimes, she must have been aware that, save as the mother of an anticipated heir, she counted for little in his life. She must further have known that all around her were cognisant of the condition of things. William Dunbar, her devoted partisan and an inveterate beggar, had enlisted her interest on his behalf

when a benefice he coveted fell vacant ; and
Margaret having failed to obtain the boon from
the King, the poet gave vent to his disappointment in verses where praise of the Queen mingled
with regret that James was not " John Thom-
son's man "—the popular term employed to
designate a husband under the influence of his
wife :

> For it micht hurt in no degre,
> That one, so fair and gude as sche,
> Throw hir vertew sic wirschip wan,
> As yow to mak Johne Thomsounis man.
>
> .   .   .   .   .
>
> The mersy of that sweit meik Rois,
> Suld soft yow, Thrissill, I suppois,
> Quhois pykis throw me so reuthles ran,
> God gif ye war Johne Thomsounis man !

It was well to be flattered by a court poet.
It was less satisfactory that the consciousness
should be brought home to the wife that she
had no power over her husband, and that she
was the object of public sympathy, if not of
pity.

Nor was James without his periods of gloom.
Remorse had not slackened its hold upon him
with time, and whilst his court was crowded
and blithe, whilst he was busy with the creation
of a navy and sought indefatigably to render

THE PALACE, STIRLING CASTLE.
Photo by Francis C. Inglis.

Scotland a maritime power, whilst all the
interests of his many-sided nature were developed and indulged, whilst he made wise
laws, attended to their administration, and
reduced his turbulent rebels to submission,
whilst too he paid his court to the women
to whom his heart was leased in turn—whilst
all this and more filled his life, there were times,
as of old, when clouds of bitter melancholy
overshadowed his spirit, and sorrow and penitence would drive him away from court and
courtiers, from the men who flattered him
and the men who loved him, and he would
seek the shrine of St. Ninian or some other
place of pilgrimage, or would bury himself in
the silence of a monastery until the dark mood
was overpast.

What the men and women he left behind on
these occasions may privately have thought
of his conduct, Dunbar again, with a poet's
licence, openly expressed, not afraid to turn into
covert ridicule the habits of his master in verses
written when James was in retirement at Stirling
and addressed to the King himself :

> We that ar heir in hevins glory,
> To yow that are in purgatory,
> Commendis ws on our hairtly wyiss ;
> I mene we folk in parradyis,

In Edinburch with all mirriness
To yow of Striuilling in distress,
Quhair nowdir plesance nor delyt is,
For pety this epistill wrytis.

Thus the ribald poem begins, where the King is entreated, in stanzas that parody the litanies of a Church of which Dunbar was a priest, to " come home and dwell no more in Stirling."

Whatever may have been her troubles, Margaret was not to be without her days of happiness. On February 21st, 1507, when she was still no more than seventeen, her first child was born and proved a boy, to be welcomed with rejoicing throughout the country and proclaimed Prince of Scotland and of the Isles. Margaret herself came near to losing her life, and her condition was considered so critical that James, according to Bishop Lesley's account, " yielding himself up to anguish, would not be soothed by any human consolation. Wherefore, since he placed all hope of his wife's recovery in God alone, he went on foot to the shrine of St. Ninian." Others aver that though Margaret recovered, and her recovery was attributed to the pilgrimage undertaken by the King, its indirect effects were not wholly to her advantage, and that it was during this absence that he renewed his acquaintance with Janet Kennedy, to the indignation of the old Earl of Angus, who ended, in spite of all, by making her his wife. The rivalry between her two lovers—young and old—appears to have been acute, if Drummond's statement, to the effect that James put Angus in confinement in the Isle of Arran " for taking Jane Kennedy out of Galloway," is justified.

The manner in which the pilgrimage had been made is another example of the singular combination of religion and pleasure, legitimate and the reverse, always to be found in James's dealings with himself. As he journeyed on foot to his goal—St. Ninian's shrine was on the Galloway coast—he was attended by four Italian minstrels ; who, unaccustomed to northern habits, were so worn out by the time the sanctuary was reached that it was necessary to procure horses to carry them back to Holyrood. When Margaret had sufficiently recovered to undertake a pilgrimage of thanksgiving to the same spot, it was accomplished in a different fashion. She made the journey in a litter, accompanied by seventeen pack-horses laden with her luggage, James bringing also on this occasion baggage enough to load three horses.

Margaret's recovery had not after all been complete ; her pleasure in her baby was marred by the condition of her own health, and for some months after the child's birth she continued, says Bishop Lesley, to be sore vexed with sickness. It was a year of signs and wonders, considered by superstitious folk as ominous. In August a star, giving light like a sunbeam, was visible in the skies for the space of twenty days, " and thereupon the King, by the counsel of some godly men, used great devotion and prayer all that time."

The year ended nevertheless without disaster, nor was it until the February of 1508 that the child whose birth had been hailed with so much rejoicing died. As Margaret mourned her first-born, it can scarcely have failed to add bitterness to her grief that James's son by Marion Boyd, Alexander—soon to be entrusted to Erasmus's care, and already addressed, by virtue of the papal bulls his father had obtained, as " my Lord of St. Andrews "—was a prominent figure at court, and filled the post of Primate of Scotland. Margaret Stewart, too, daughter of Margaret Drummond, had been brought to Edinburgh, was openly acknowledged by James as his daughter, and was afterwards, when she was sixteen or seventeen, married to the son and heir of the Earl of Huntley.

The King's absences were becoming more frequent and prolonged ; and though his wife may have been learning to adapt herself to circumstances it is a significant fact that the children who had made their home at Stirling—the death of one of whom had coincided with the wedding festivities—were now, on Margaret's visiting the Castle, removed first to a lodging in the town, and were then placed permanently at the episcopal palace of St. Andrews, where they received the visits of their father. Stirling was the Queen's dower castle, and she may justly have objected to the presence there of its former occupants.

Some time before the birth of his son James had contemplated a more prolonged absence from court and wife than was involved in his periods of seclusion or his visits to the more distant parts of his kingdom. The intention he had announced of undertaking a pilgrimage to the Holy Land has been ascribed to more than one motive. Generosity carried to excess, the magnificence of the arrangements at court, the sums spent in shipbuilding, and the like causes, had involved him in financial difficulties from which it was hard to find a way of escape. New taxes were invented, borne by the nation with a patience proving its love for the ruler who imposed them; but the drain upon the national resources was so severe and the King's straits were so great that Drummond, writing of the final catastrophe, goes so far as to say that "death seemed to have come to him wishedly and in good time." It may be doubted whether money complications would have led James to desire an end to life; but it was certainly necessary in the interests alike of King and kingdom to devise some method of reducing expenditure; and to the need of economy the intended journey to Palestine has been attributed by some writers. Nor is it unlikely that it had its share in recommending a project due in the first place to the motives professed by James—to religious fervour and a desire to expiate the guilt of which the burden never ceased to oppress him.

His intention was announced at home and abroad; Venice was solicited to supply galleys as means of transport, and the Pope was begged to excuse him if he failed to visit Rome on his way. In Scotland the suggestion seems to have been received with favour, and many men

STIRLING CASTLE.
From an old print.

188]

" as if bound by a vow " allowed their hair and beards to grow.[1]

To James's adventurous spirit the prospect of a journey to lands unknown would have presented powerful attractions, independently of its devotional aspect. That his knowledge of geography was limited may be inferred from a letter to the King of Denmark, where he observes that, though the gypsies in Scotland appeared to him to be good Christians, King John would be better acquainted with them than himself, as his kingdom lay so much nearer to Egypt than his own The projected expedition to the East would therefore offer the additional charm conferred by a large degree of uncertainty as to its conditions and scope. His purpose was not destined to be carried into effect. His presence was required at home, and the moment never arrived when he was at liberty to leave the kingdom to itself for an indefinite period. But he was haunted to the end by the desire to make the pilgrimage, and so well was this understood by his people that when he had gone the ultimate journey from which there is no return it was believed by many that their lost King had taken his way to the Holy Land, there to perform his vow.

[1] Buchanan.

CHAPTER XIII

1508

Quarrels with England—Arran a prisoner—Wolsey's mission
—D'Aubigny at Edinburgh—His death—James's shipbuilding and its results—The family of Bartons.

In the year 1508 the "perpetual peace" between England and Scotland was once more
endangered. The habits of centuries are not
discarded in a moment ; and though the two
heads of the rival kingdoms might have pledged
themselves to amity, their turbulent subjects
were not willing to forgo at once their custom
and their pastime of warfare.

Whilst each party conceived that they
had reason for complaining of the other, and
skirmishes and breaches of the peace on the
Border were of frequent occurrence, a more
serious cause of resentment on James's part
was supplied by the detention of his cousin,
the Earl of Arran, as a captive in England.

The relations of Scotland and France and their traditional friendship were ever a source of disquiet to those whose interest it was to maintain a balance of power in Europe, and to the fact that Arran and his brother, Sir Patrick Hamilton, had been spending some time at the French court, a political significance was liable to be attached. Henry's anger had further been roused by the breach of the articles of the treaty between England and Scotland committed by the brothers in passing through his territory without licence or safe-conduct asked or obtained. His displeasure took the form of placing both Hamiltons in confinement. The younger brother was speedily released and suffered to continue his journey homewards ; but Arran, as the culprit of greater importance, was retained a prisoner ; whilst James's natural indignation at the step was increased by the accounts, true or false, brought by Sir Patrick, of the scurvy treatment to which his brother and the King's kinsman were subjected.

Henry, his drastic measure notwithstanding, had no desire to proceed to extremities or to break the peace with Scotland, and in March 1508 he despatched an envoy—Thomas Wolsey,

the future cardinal[1]—to explain the circumstances to his son-in-law. The rough draft
of a lengthy report drawn up by the ambassador gives an account of his reception at
court, and of the disturbed state of James's
mind and temper at the time.

It augured ill for the success of a pacific mission that the envoy was kept waiting five days
before he was so much as accorded an audience
by the King. James was said to be busy
" making gunpowder," and in spite of the
Queen's great labours and the ambassador's
solicitations, he could not, or would not, spare
the time to receive his father-in-law's representative. When the interview at length took
place, he was plainly in no placable mood.
Letters had been sent by Henry, who had
assumed the tone of the person aggrieved and
had complained that many Scots, some of them
being great personages and others in " dis-
sembled habits " or disguises, had made their
way through his dominions without licence or
safe-conduct. In some cases, it was added,
ambassadors from princes with whom Henry

---

[1] Pinkerton believed the envoy to have been Dr. West,
but Mr. Gairdner has good reason to conclude that he was
mistaken.

was not on friendly terms had been secretly
conveyed through his territory. These letters
were produced, and supplied matter of discussion, stress being laid by James upon
trivial points of disagreement between their
wording and the envoy's verbal report. To
the charge that foreigners had been smuggled
through the country he apparently pleaded
guilty in the case of the ambassadors of his
cousin, the Duke of Gueldres, but in no other.
The troubles on the Border were also discussed.
The true grievance, however, was undoubtedly
Arran's detention, felt by James, not without
justice, to be a personal affront, and resented
by him as such.

"As touching the Earl of Arran," wrote
Wolsey, "this thing that the King of Scots
taketh greatly to heart, and all the great men
of his realm ; for though so be the said Earl . . .
for causes by me rehearsed deserved punishment, yet the King of Scots said that herein
your Grace hath dealt very unkindly, forasmuch
as the doing of the Earl was contrary to his
mind and otherwise than he commanded him."
Had Henry acted as a loving father, he would
have made his complaint to James, and James
would have taken the punishment of Arran

13

upon himself. The terms offered by Henry by way of propitiation constituted an additional offence ; since he proposed to release the young Earl on condition that he promised in writing and upon oath to return to England should Henry demand it. " To this the King of Scots saith that if the Earl make any such oath or seal to return, he shall hang him at his entry into Scotland. . . . I cannot by no means induce him to grant the said bond and oath. . . . I perceive that he would very gladly that the Earl should come ; howbeit he is stiff-hearted, that he will not make intercession for his deliverance."

An aggravation of the indignity put upon James had been contained in a message from the French ambassador in London to the effect that if the King would write and ask him to desire Henry to set Arran free, he did not doubt that the thing would be done. James was in no wise grateful for the proffer of the Frenchman's good offices.

" The King of Scots," wrote Wolsey, " would be right loath that any stranger should be mean betwixt your Grace and him. In this thing resteth, as I perceive, the weight of all."

Wolsey's mission was rendered yet more difficult owing to the condition of public opinion in Scotland. It was true that James professed that he valued Henry's friendship and goodwill more than that of any other prince. So long as his wife's father treated him as a son, he would be ready to live and die with him, against all others, even were the French nation included. On the other hand the whole of Scotland, nobles and commons alike, were vehemently in favour of a renewal of the ancient league with France. " There be no more that sticketh in this matter," explained the envoy, " but only the King, the Queen, and the Bishop of Moray. As he (the King) saith, there was never man worse welcome into Scotland than I, forasmuch as they think I am come to let the renewal of the league betwixt Scotland and France. They keep their matters so secret here," added Wolsey contemptuously, " that the wives in the market-place knoweth every cause of my coming."

With the King he flattered himself that he had made some way. Bernard d'Aubigny, a Scot by extraction, resident in France, was expected in Scotland, with the ostensible object of visiting the shrine of St. Ninian ; but, as it was more than suspected, on a mission from his master ; and James promised Wolsey to send the Bishop of Moray to make known to Henry his purpose in coming. The Bishop was also to carry with him an autograph letter from James containing secrets to be revealed to none but Henry.

Though in the ambassador's opinion the heart of the King of Scots had been wonderfully mollified, the fact that his cousin was not set at liberty till towards the close of the year may conceivably have weakened the effect of the envoy's diplomacy.

Close upon the Englishman's departure came the arrival of the French ambassador, who now appeared to have been commissioned by Louis XII to obtain James's advice as to the disposal of his daughter's hand. Should he give her in marriage to the Duc d'Angoulême, notwithstanding the fact that Charles, King of Castile, was also her suitor ? On this important point Louis showed a flattering desire to consult James. The King's answer was prompt. Louis, he said, had, he knew, counsel enough ; yet since he put the question to him, he would do better, in his opinion, to marry his daughter in his own realm and with him who should succeed him than to bestow her on a foreign prince.

Meantime d'Aubigny had been given a warm welcome. A soldier with a brilliant record, James was eager to do him honour ; messengers were sent to warn the nobles of his visit, and jousts and tournaments were arranged to grace the occasion.

Proud of his guest, a Scot though in the service of the French King, James " treated him very gently," set him ever at his own table, constituted him judge in all the jousts, and named him, in recognition of his achievements in the field, " the father of wars."

Nor was the King content, when feats of arms were to be performed, to be a mere looker-on. In the course of the tournament, an unknown cavalier rode into the lists, calling himself the Wild Knight, and attended by an escort in savage array. After overthrowing the Frenchmen who contested the field with him and being awarded the prize, he discarded his incognito, and was seen to be the King. And thus was the French ambassador welcomed to Edinburgh.

His coming had a melancholy sequel. Scarcely were the festivities at an end when they were succeeded by the death of the man in whose honour they had taken place. His mission, whatever had been its true purpose, was left incomplete, his private pilgrimage unmade ; and only the heart of the French Scot was carried to the shrine of St. Ninian.

A more personal sorrow was soon to overtake the King. Close upon the court merrymaking came the birth and death of yet another child—a little daughter—and the dangerous illness of the Queen, her mother. And James, brooding over his repeated domestic misfortunes, wondered whether the loss of his children was a judgment upon him for his conduct to his father, and remorse again stabbed at his heart.

Whatever else was going on at court or in the kingdom, there was one subject from which James's attention was never long diverted. Shipbuilding, under his personal supervision, went on apace. The results were not always favourable to peace. If it was well to make Scotland a maritime power, it was practically certain that her exploits in this direction would involve her in conflict with other nations. There were old-standing quarrels which Scotland had hitherto failed to settle

and which she was now placed in a position
to revive ; there were ancient grudges to be
avenged, and well-remembered grievances to
be redressed. As early as 1506 there had been
trouble with Holland, when, angered at damage
inflicted upon Scottish shipping by Dutch
vessels, James placed Andrew Barton in command of " a great and costly ship " he had
just built, with full permission to use it
against the Dutch robbers. Barton performed
his duty with marked success. Many Dutch
vessels were seized, and the heads of Hollanders,
taken and slain, were sent, ghastly trophies,
home in casks to the King.

Reprisals undertaken in consequence of Portuguese misdeeds were a more serious business.
Long ago, in the year 1476, a Scottish ship
laden with merchandise and commanded by
John Barton, father to Andrew, had been
captured by the Portuguese. No opportunity
of vengeance had offered at the time ; thirty
years had gone by and compensation had not
been obtained. James now determined to take
the law into his own hands, and letters of mark
or reprisal were granted to the three sons of
the old sea captain, Andrew, Robert, and John,
who were thereby empowered to seize all Portu-

guese vessels, until such time as 12,000 ducats should have been recovered. These letters, bearing the date of November 1506, opened out a fair prospect of future hostilities. The Bartons were, with the exception of Wood, the most skilled and famous of Scottish seamen, and could be trusted to make the most of the facilities afforded them. It is a significant fact that, as early as 1508 and again in 1511, Robert Barton was acquiring lands, becoming in the end a man of wealth and property, and that in 1510 his brother Andrew was also numbered amongst landed proprietors. It was not until 1563 that the letters of mark granted to the Barton family were revoked by Mary, as having been turned to the purpose of piracy—which was indeed more than likely.

By some punctilious persons even the earlier exploits of the three brothers were considered to savour of freebooting. In 1508 Robert Barton had come near to falling a victim to a misapprehension of this nature on the part of the magistrates of Veere, in the island of Walcheren. Having been taken captive and brought before them, he would have run the risk of ending his career by means of the gallows had not his master promptly intervened and been so successful in the vindication of his sea-captain that Barton was permitted to escape. As the King further explained in a letter addressed to Maximilian, so far from being guilty of piracy, the seaman had done no more than execute justice.

James's chief achievement in the matter of shipbuilding belongs to 1511. The *St. Michael*—" a very monstrous great ship "— was completed in the course of this year, and had taken so much timber in the building that not only all the woods in Fife, save one, had been laid waste, but material was imported from Norway besides. Her length was 240 feet, she was 36 feet broad, and her sides were 10 feet thick within walls of oak. " She cumbered all Scotland," says Lindsay, " to get her to the sea," and when she was committed to the sea and under sail it was computed that she had cost the King £40,000. Captain Andrew Wood was her captain, and Robert Barton—rescued from the gallows—master skipper. " If any man believes," adds Lindsay, " that this ship was not as we have shown, let him pass to the place of Tullibardine, where he will find the breadth and length of her set with hawthorn ; as for my author was Captain Andrew Wood, principal captain of her, and Robert Barton, who was master skipper."

The King had watched over the building of the great ship with the keenest interest. When, finished, she lay in the roads he paid her daily visits, often dining and supping on board, and exhibiting her to the lords and nobles he brought with him.

Yet his very labours in the strengthening of his power on the seas contributed to lead up to the catastrophe that was ever drawing nearer.

CHAPTER XIV

1509—1512

THE death of Henry VII, in April 1509, was
to have a disastrous effect upon the relations
of England and Scotland. The dead King
had been a cautious man, and had besides an
eye to economy. For both reasons war would
have been distasteful to him. He would in
especial have regretted a breach with the
husband of the little daughter whom he had
not seen since he had sent her, a child, to her
northern home.

His son was cast in a different mould ; he
was hot-tempered and masterful, with "a
brutal force and an iron resolution which gave
him the advantage over the sensitive and

romantic King of Scots." [1] It will be recalled
that anger at Margaret's betrothal to the
traditional enemy of his country had been such
as to throw the boy of eleven into a fever, and
now at eighteen the recollection of the sister
who had quitted England six years earlier
had become one of the blurred and indistinct
memories of his childhood.

At first all went well, and sanguine
persons might have hoped that the change
in the sovereignty of England would leave
the Scottish alliance undisturbed. Bishop
Forman went backwards and forwards, with
a commission to arrange for the observance
and renewal of the treaty of amity, doubtless
gleaning some personal advantage from the
performance of his good offices ; and letters
overflowing with expressions of affection and
confidence passed between the two Kings.

"Dearest brother and cousin," wrote James,
"we have received your loving letters written
with your hand, where through we understand
the good and kind heart ye bear on to us, of the
which we are right glad, considering our tenderness of blood."

Peace therefore continued for the present

[1] P. Hume Brown, *History of Scotland.*

HENRY VIII.
From the painting at Windsor Castle.

between the two countries. Whilst public affairs
prospered, private sorrows had again overshadowed the Scottish Court. Another son,
named Arthur—perhaps after the Queen's dead
brother, perhaps after James's favourite hero,
the King of old—had been born in October
1509. Once more an heir to the throne had
received a royal welcome. The child had
lived for nine months, but in July 1510 he had
gone the way of his little forerunners and again
the Holyrood nurseries were empty. As James
mourned his loss in the seclusion at Stirling
which he had sought, accompanied on this
occasion by the Queen, the old sense of chastisement for personal guilt, never long slumbering,
the old desire of expiating it by a pilgrimage
to the Holy Land, re-awakened ; and, though
it was impossible to carry the project into
effect at the time, the thought of it did not
cease to be present with him.

However it may have been with the childless
mother, to the King the return of his son, the
brilliant young Archbishop of St. Andrews,
his studies at Padua and elsewhere completed,
may have brought some consolation. From
Erasmus's description of the boy who had been
placed for a time under his care, it would seem

that Alexander Stewart had inherited to a full degree the gifts of the race whose blood ran in his veins.

" I once lived with the King's son in the city of Sens," wrote Erasmus, " and I there taught him rhetoric and Greek. Heavens ! how quick, how attentive, how eager he was ; how many things could he undertake together." The mornings were devoted to serious studies ; " he gave his afternoons to music, to the monochord, flute, or lute ; and he sometimes sang while playing on a stringed instrument. Even at mealtime he was not forgetful of his studies. The chaplain always read some good book . . . nor was the reader interrupted, except when some of the doctors among whom he sat suggested aught, or when he made inquiry about something that he did not clearly understand. On the other hand, he liked tales, when they were brief and when they treated of literary matters. . . . If he had any spare time he spent it in reading history, for in that he took extreme delight. Thus it was that, though he was a youth scarcely eighteen years old, he excelled as much in every kind of learning as in all those qualities which we admire in a man."

This was the lad who had returned to Scotland

to be "thankfully received by the King and nobles, principally because he had exercised his youthhead so well in letters and virtue." It is to be inferred, by his presence on the field of Flodden, that neither had the profession of arms been neglected. It cannot have been more than three years after the time of which Erasmus wrote that he was called upon to lament the fate of the pupil whose gifts he had described. "What," he asked mournfully, "hadst thou to do with Mars, of all the gods of the poets the most infatuate—thou, who wert the disciple of the Muses and of Christ?"

With the serious exception of the lack of an heir all might have seemed to prosper with James until the year 1511. It was at this time that clouds began to gather on the horizon.

The league of Cambrai, by which Pope Julius, Ferdinand of Aragon, Louis of France and Maximilian of Austria had been united against Venice, formed as early as 1508, had involved neither Henry nor James in war. Neither would feel called upon to interfere in the affairs of Italy or for the protection of the Venetian republic. It was another matter when Julius, become desirous of expelling foreigners from the peninsula and jealous in particular of the acquisitions of the French, succeeded in banding together against Louis his late allies and in including Henry VIII in the " Holy League." The fact that the majority of the great Powers of Europe were now combined to effect the overthrow of Scotland's traditional friend roused James to indignant protest, and disposed him to throw himself into the fray.

Other causes, trivial in themselves, contributed to render the relations of the brothers-in-law strained. Prince Arthur, dying, had bequeathed to his sister a legacy, consisting of " silver work and golden pieces, rings, chains, and precious stones." So far none of these treasures had been delivered over to Margaret ; whether, as some have surmised, that they had been left to the Prince's father for his life, or because Henry VII had been loath that they should leave the country. It was, at all events, only after her father's death that Margaret appears to have urged her claims to her brother's legacy. But though fair answers were returned by Henry to her representations, the property was not made over to its lawful owner, and the fact that it was unfairly with-held was not unlikely to lessen the Queen's zeal in forwarding her brother's interests in Scotland.

There is no doubt, however, that what influence she possessed was exerted in favour of peace, and that the promises contained in a letter written to Ferdinand of Aragon were sincere. " We have willingly heard," she wrote in Latin, " what your orator has told us, and have repeated it to the King our husband. But he was already persuaded and wishes nothing so much as peace amongst Christian princes, and ceases not to exhort the Pope on the one hand, and the King of France on the other, thereto ; inviting to the same our dearest brother, your Highness's son "—Henry was by this time married to Katharine of Aragon— " as your Highness will understand from your orator."

James might wish for peace. It was clearly to Henry's interest to leave no enemy behind when he was quitting his kingdom to conduct a campaign abroad ; but events were constantly occurring with a tendency to render a pacific policy on the part of the two sovereigns difficult to carry out. Prior to the death of Henry VII, troubles on the Border had culminated in the murder of Sir

14

Robert Ker, who, as Warden of the Middle
Marches, had been present at a meeting designed to adjust the recurrent grievances of the
district. Ker, a man to whom James was
personally attached, was assassinated by three
Englishmen, of whom one alone was delivered
up to justice, the other two making good, for
the time, their escape. The matter could not
be allowed to rest; James was urgent in his
complaints, and in 1511 a second murderer
was summarily dealt with by the vassals of
the son and successor of the dead man. But
Heron, the chief criminal, was still at large, and
James persisted in his protests. He was clearly
within his rights in demanding the punishment
of the offender; and Henry, anxious to avoid
a breach, sent ambassadors in November to
offer compensation; but no solid agreement
was arrived at. If Henry continued to slay
and imprison Scottish subjects, war would be
the sole issue—so James told the Pope in a
letter of December. He was also firm in de-
claring that whilst England was leagued with
the enemies of France no satisfactory arrangement could be made. A letter was sent to
Henry himself by the usual intermediary,
Bishop Forman. The Bishop, wrote James,

loved the observation of the perpetual peace,
"and now we have sent him unto you for a
final conclusion, redress, and reformation to be
had of all ruptures and attempts done on both
the borders . . . and for good rule to be put
thereupon in time to come." Would James's
dearest brother and cousin co-operate with
Forman in these matters, as in other great
matters—probably the Holy League—which
he was commissioned to discuss?

The troubles on the Border had not been the
sole causes of quarrel during this year; other
events had taken place in August rendering any true pacification more difficult than
before. His navy was very near James's heart;
and a sea fight in which one of his best-loved
captains, Andrew Barton, had been worsted
and slain by Lord Thomas Howard roused
him to hot indignation.

It was again a moot question whether Barton
was not, in the character of a pirate, fair prey. It
was alleged that merchants of all nations were
attacked by him and that when he robbed the
English he was accustomed to assert that they
were Portuguese. Exasperated by tales such as
these, Henry had despatched the two Howards,
Thomas and Edmund, Surrey's sons, to seek

and chastise the marauder. This was promptly done. Lying off the Downs, Lord Thomas, Lord Admiral of England—separated for the moment from his brother—caught sight of Barton sailing towards Scotland, gave him chase and overtook him. A battle followed, and in the end the English were victorious; Andrew Barton, already wounded to death, was captured, and both the *Lion*, commanded by him in person, and his second ship, the *Jenny Pirwin*, were taken and towed in as prizes to the Thames.

It was no wonder that James, at these tidings, was "wonderful wroth." The English admiral had, according to the view he took of the affair, been guilty of a distinct breach of the peace; and he wrote to Henry demanding compensation. Henry, in reply, enumerated the misdeeds of Andrew Barton; affirmed that it did not become one prince to charge another with breaking a league because justice had been done upon pirate or thief, and took credit to himself for the mercy shown to the crews, whom he had released and sent home.

There was something to be said for Henry's argument; but with Ker murdered on the Border and Barton killed at sea, James could not be expected to be in a placable mood or disposed to consider the matter coolly or impartially.

The spring of 1512 brought him a domestic happiness. Both he and the Queen were eagerly anxious to possess an heir, and Margaret, though less inclined to place faith in religious observances than her husband, had made a pilgrimage to St. Duthac's at Tain, James's own birthplace—a shrine for which he cherished a special devotion—during the summer of 1511, in the hope of obtaining a son as an answer to prayer. James, for his part, had summoned a soothsayer named "Liddell, the prophet," to Holyrood and held a private conference with him, in case he might be able to throw some light on future events. When it became known that once more a child was to be born, the anxiety felt was great. Would he see the light, as the rest had done, only to die ? Christmas was passed in unusual quiet at the palace, and as Easter drew near the court removed to Linlithgow, where the birth was to take place. The loan of "St. Margaret's sark" was obtained—a relic credited with the possession of properties appropriate to the occasion—and the result of care and prayer

and devotion was eagerly awaited. On Easter
Eve Margaret was safely delivered of a son—a
child who, though delicate, was destined to live,
and who was, in scarcely more than eighteen
months, to succeed to his father as James V.

In joy and gladness the King wrote to an-
nounce the birth to his cousin, the King of
Denmark. "On holy Easter Eve," he wrote,
"our most beloved spouse was delivered of a
son, who was presented at the font on the very
day of the Feast of the Lord's Resurrection,
and received the sign of baptism from the
priest. He gives promise of health and of
succeeding after us. It seemed proper for us
to inform your Majesty, inasmuch as he will
none the less be—provided he be spared—a
source of strength and a help to you and to us."

Save for the birth of his heir, 1512 passed on
the whole uneventfully for James. Nevertheless, looking back it is easy to see that fate was
at work preparing for the catastrophe of the
following year. Envoys from abroad visited the
Scottish court, and showed the importance
attached on the Continent to the action of the
northern King. In Europe the Holy League
was proving successful. After hard fighting,
the French had been driven out of Italy, and

Julius had had the satisfaction of seeing, in his own language, the barbarians chased beyond the Alps. Henry's part in the European contest had been less satisfactory. Bent upon the recovery of the French province, Guienne, to which the English laid claim, Henry had sent a force to Fontarabia, only to find that he had been made a tool of by his father-in-law, Ferdinand of Aragon, and used to facilitate the conquest, by Spain, of Navarre. So far, therefore, he had reaped no benefit from his interposition in European affairs and, high-spirited and inclined towards war, he was not disposed to accept his failure without an effort to retrieve it.

In the meantime, the Pope having got what he desired, had sent an envoy, Olearius, to Edinburgh to request that James would lend his assistance towards the pacification of Europe —a singular request to proceed from the man who had been so active in the promotion of war. In James's answer his smouldering irritation with regard to England was apparent. Henry, he said, constituted the principal obstacle in the way of the peace that Julius professed to desire, having made war upon France and inflicted all manner of injuries upon himself.

The question of Prince Arthur's legacy also remained unsettled. In May ambassadors from England, Lord Dacre and Dr. West, arrived with the professed purpose of removing all causes, great or small, of dissension, and it would have been wise had they been empowered to satisfy Margaret on this point. That such was Lord Dacre's opinion is plain from a letter he wrote to the Bishop of Durham on his return home. "I perceive well," he said, "that the King taketh great grudge because the Queen's duty of legacy is withholden from her; he says it is done in malice of him. No displeasure to the King's (Henry's) Grace, meseems it were honourable she were contented therein, considering the sum is so small."

This legacy was a constant and recurrent cause of dispute; and it appears from Lindsay of Pitscottie that, at some uncertain date, Bishop Forman was sent to England to endeavour to obtain it. Though the answer made by Henry to Forman's demand doubtless owes something to the imagination of the chronicler—always inclined to magnify the Bishop's successes—it may be approximately true. According to this report, the King replied that his sister should receive not only what had been

bequeathed to her, but the double thereof—
on certain conditions. " Therefore make you
memorial of all your desires, the number and
value thereof, and you shall not have the single,
but the double thereof, as I am a true prince "—
then followed the gist of the message—" on
condition that the King of Scotland will keep
his oath and bond to me . . . that never none
of us thall invade one another for no man's
pleasure, but shall live in peace and rest as
other Christian men and good neighbours should
do.   Therefore I will desire the King of Scotland,
for Almighty God's sake, that he will sit at home
in his own chair, and let me and the King of
France part between us to seek the right of my
own pension, which is holden from me wrongly
by the pride and avarice of France. . . ."   If
James would do this, no question of gold, land,
or riches should come between them.

   To sit at home in his chair and permit his ally
to be attacked was not a condition James would
be inclined to observe ; and for the present the
legacy remained in Henry's hands. Yet what
he demanded was not unreasonable, since in
the treaty of peace between England and Scotland, by which both nations were still bound, it
was specially enacted that though either King

might give aid to an ally, it was not to be by an invasion of the other's territories. In lending assistance to France either by sea or abroad, James would therefore not have infringed the pledges contained in the treaty. By the invasion of England those pledges were clearly broken, and the treaty brought to an end. By another article it had been enacted that he who should break the treaty of peace was to be excommunicated, a proviso which was subsequently carried out with regard to James.

At the Scottish court it was suspected that the true object of the envoys sent to Edinburgh was to keep Robert Barton and his ships at home until the English fleet should have crossed unmolested over to France. They appear to have got scanty satisfaction out of their visit—more especially as almost corresponding in date with it was one from de la Motte, ambassador from France, who had met and encountered an English fleet on his way, had sunk three vessels and brought seven others captive to Leith.

De la Motte had a definite aim—viz., to press upon James war with Henry. He further brought ample promises of money and munitions of war. These supplies were indeed necessary. Scottish finance was at a low ebb, and in the following September a letter from one Ainslow to the Bishop of Durham stated that the King had engaged to make war upon England, provided Louis would transfer to him the tribute he had been wont to pay to the English sovereign. Otherwise he had no money to make war withal.

De la Motte obtained what he sought. The ancient league between Scotland and France was renewed, binding James to take part against every foe who attacked his ally, and yet another step was taken by the King upon the road which was leading him to his destruction.

CHAPTER XV

1513

Dr. West at the Scottish court—His reports to Henry VIII
—Unsatisfactory results of his mission—Margaret's letter
to her brother.

THE year 1513 was come—a year destined to
prove disastrous to Scotland. Yet at Holyrood there must have been rejoicing. The
little heir was well and thriving. "I hear
say," Lindsay reports Henry VIII as observing,
"Margaret, my eldest sister, has an heir
male of good expectation," praying God to
bless him and keep him from his enemies.
The English King being as yet childless, his
sister's son was now second in succession to
the English throne and as such of importance
to both countries.

The two courts were still on terms of nominal
amity, though all men must have been aware
how hollow was their friendship and how
precarious the peace that formally existed.

Messengers went to and fro in the fruitless
endeavour to amend the condition of veiled
hostility that prevailed or at least to avert a
definite breach. In March Dr. West paid
another visit to Scotland ; and through his
detailed dispatches the court and the King
are again thrown into vivid relief.

From Stirling, whither he had first repaired,
he wrote that for a week—it was Passion-tide—
the King had been secluded in the monastery
of the Friars Observant, and that no access
could be had to him. On Good Friday, April
24th, the ambassador, who had arrived the day
before, attended the service in the royal chapel,
and was summoned when it was over to the
Queen's private seat, to receive her welcome
and to give her tidings of her brother and
sister. " And when she had read your letters,"
West told Henry, " I delivered her your Grace's
token and the Princess's, which she received
with such manner I cannot declare unto your
Grace, it was so joyfully and lovingly received ;
saying these words, ' If I were now in my great
sickness again, this were enough to make me
whole,' seeing that your Grace did so remember
her."

On the following day, Easter Eve, there was

no meeting—"that day," wrote West, "I came not at the court, as my servants were busy also to serve God "—but on Sunday he was invited to dine with the Queen, and the time at dinner passed very joyously, whilst Margaret made inquiries as to the brother she had left a child—" of his stature and goodly personage," and his occupations.

After dinner the conversation took a less satisfactory turn. West informed the Queen that his master was to cross the sea, with his army, into France, " wherewith she was right heavy." The envoy also reminded her that she had been sent to Scotland as a messenger of peace and exhorted her to use her influence to induce her husband to refrain from hostilities during Henry's absence, obtaining her promise to do what she could in the matter. After which Margaret had claims of her own to press.

There was still a question pending with regard to a legacy left to the Queen, whether by this was meant Prince Arthur's bequest, already the subject of so much discussion, or some further sum of money to which Margaret was entitled under her father's will ; and she proceeded to question West with regard to the payment of it, asking whether it had been sent her by

MARGARET TUDOR, QUEEN OF SCOTLAND.
From a painting at Hampton Court Palace.

Henry. The doctor had, in point of fact, the bone of contention with him ; but his instructions were only to hand it over upon certain conditions, and so he told her.

" I said yea, which I was ready to deliver her, so the King would promise to keep the treaty of peace, and she asked, ' And not else ? ' And I said no, for if he would make war, your Grace would not only withhold that, but also take from them the best towns they had. And or I had fully finished this sentence, the King came upon us, and so we broke communication for that time ; and after some communication for a pastime had, he went to the sermon ; and that done, I departed for that night."

It was fortunate, in the interests of peace, that James had not heard the doctor's unconciliatory reply to his wife's demand. Margaret, anxious for amity between her husband and her brother, was not likely to repeat it.

On the following day West was again at court, accompanied on this occasion by Ramsay, Henry VII's spy, who was probably continuing his good offices to his son. Before High Mass the envoy was summoned by James to his " travers," or private latticed seat, in the chapel, and had a conversation with him in which sundry

briefs and bulls of the late Pope—Julius had
died in February—were discussed. Both Julius
and his successor, Leo X, had shown themselves
Henry's warm partisans and the papal reprobation of James's conduct towards England was
shortly to culminate in the sentence of excommunication under which he died. Having been
ever loyal to the Church, the King was naturally
sore and angry, and his disposition was far from
docile. Laying the blame for the papal attitude
upon the Cardinal of York and on information
supplied by Henry and his Council, " he said,"
pursued West, " he would appeal from it, and
send the Bishop of Moray to Rome for the
same, and to do his obedience to the new
Pope." Were he disposed to make war, he
would not tarry on account of the Pope's
monition—so he told West. ". . . And I said
I was sure that there was no sentence given
against him, but under condition that he broke
the peace . . . and that therefore there was
nothing innovated that should need such appeal.
And also I said I knew not to whom he should
appeal; and he answered laughing that he
would appeal to Prester John. . . ."

Some concessions West appears to have obtained. James declared that he would not

make war on England without first sending a
herald to inform Henry of it, so that should he
be in France, he might return to the defence
of his kingdom.   But on the whole the negotiations did not prosper.   To the offer of a thousand marks made by the envoy in compensation
for all claims, the King answered with scorn
that he did not want money and would not sell
his gear.   He also repeated a report, solemnly
denied by West, that Henry had named a
successor to the English crown—a proceeding
prejudicial to his own rights.   Still persisting in
his design of visiting Jerusalem, he urged that
the expedition could only be performed with
Louis's help.   "A little book of four sheets"
was produced, signed and sealed by the French
King, and containing various promises and
pledges on his part; the tenth of Louis's revenues
were to be levied by James himself, and a
certain number of men-at-arms and of shipping
to be provided to convey him on his way.   In
return, James was asked to do what was possible
to make peace.

"This read, the King said to me, 'Now you
see wherefore I favour the French King and
wherefore I am loath to lose him; for if I do,
I shall be never able to perform my journey.'"

15

To which West could only reply by throwing doubt upon the keeping of Louis's fair promises. When the ambassador pressed the true object of his mission, namely, to obtain an undertaking from James that he would observe the peace in Henry's absence, the King's answer was ambiguous. If Henry would keep the peace, so would he ; but he declined to put any pledge into writing ; Henry should have no letter of his, no new bond which might be shown in France and make trouble for him with the King. He knew his own mind well enough. Whereupon West replied that he now perceived that he, for his part, knew neither the King nor his mind, " wherewith he was sore moved and chafed mightily."

Thus the fruitless wrangles went on from day to day, continually covering the same ground. According to the view taken by West, James, with the object of saving appearances with regard to France, spoke more sharply when his lords were present than when he was alone with the envoy. Should England make him similar promises to those of Louis, he told West, or so the doctor reported, that he cared not to keep him. If the words were correctly repeated; they do not tally with the

determination displayed by James throughout
to adhere at all costs to his bond with the
French King, and his recurrent demand that
Henry should refrain from attacking him.
On this point all the negotiations hinged.
When the singular request was preferred that
he would grant Henry the loan of the apple
of his eye, the great *St. Michael*, the King's
reply was to the effect that if he would make
peace with France he might command all his
ships.

The legacy left to the Queen remained a
lesser matter of dispute. Henry's offer to pay
it over on condition that his demands were
granted was treated by James with anger and
contempt. The Queen, he said, should lose
nothing for his sake—he would make the payment to her himself : " Ye may do to your
own as you think best," he wrote to her brother
a week or two later, " she shall have no loss
thereof." He was not a man to allow money to
weigh in an affair of honour.

West was not unnaturally growing weary
of a mission which he must have perceived had
little chance of success. The entire nation was
in favour of the French alliance and was hostile
to the English representative, and the doctor

disliked his position. " I had liefer your Grace had commanded me to tarry so long in Turkey," he complained, " this country is so miserable, and the people so ungracious ; and over that I shall have scant money to bring me home, the country is so dear."

From Stirling the court moved to Edinburgh, and the envoy with it ; writing thence, a fortnight later, that preparations for war went on, and that de la Motte, Louis's ambassador, was expected to arrive and to bring provisions for the fleet.

With James he continued to have heated discussions, confessing that little satisfaction was to be obtained from the King. Neither could he get his business done, so as to enable him to start on his way homewards. He was, he complained, driven forth with words—his true grievance being that he was not driven forth, but was detained. He wanted letters for his master as the result of his labours ; and though James would not have objected to give him letters, they were such that he had refused to be the bearer of them. They had contained nothing regarding the peace, which had been the main reason of his coming, and had only dealt with Henry's " unkindnesses."

One subject of satisfaction to the discontented doctor was the brief addressed by the late Pope to Henry—so joyous and comfortable to him that he could not express it. Recurring to it, James had observed that Henry had been fortunate in having a Pope so favourable to him. The King's secretary too expressed his opinion that this brief had done more damage to kindness and amity between the two sovereigns than all the French ambassadors. It is clear that James resented it bitterly. "As touching this same point," wrote West, "the King said once to me that, if the Pope had lived and there had been but three Bishops that had kept a Council, he would have been with them against the Pope. Howbeit, I suppose it was but a crak" (boast).

From West's point of view—that of a peace ambassador—his protracted stay at James's court must have been purely futile, and he was eager to be gone. Repeated conferences brought the matter in question no further forward ; James obstinately declined to put what West desired into writing ; not only because he feared to imperil his relations with France, but because he had taken umbrage at an assertion made by Henry, to the effect that his words and deeds did not agree. Yet he was a man of curious and changing moods, and there were moments when a desire for cordiality with his wife's brother appeared to stir within him. Thus to an attempt on West's part to prove that his master's friendship would, if forfeited, be a greater loss than that of Louis, he replied that though he did not flatter with words, Henry should find him good in deeds, and he would rather die with him than see him dishonoured.

When at length the ambassador received permission to depart, James dismissed him "with good will" and sent him to take farewell of the Queen at Linlithgow, where she then was with her little son. She had, the King said, tokens to send to her brother and his wife. On a Sunday afternoon, therefore, West rode thither, reaching the palace by four o'clock, and was introduced at once into Margaret's presence. The Queen asked what answer he was taking back from James, and hearing that nothing satisfactory had been committed to writing, she said—what West already knew—that the King was afraid lest it should be shown in France.

"And I answered that then he stood in great

QUEEN MARGARET'S BOWER, LINLITHGOW PALACE.
Photo by Francis C. Inglis.

awe of France, if he durst not show in writing that he would keep that thing that he was sworn to for fear of France."

Margaret could only reply that she was right sorry, and, according to West, admitted that Henry was now in the right and the King in the wrong. She had done all that was in her power, and she took leave of the envoy, sending him to see the infant prince before he left, whom he found " a right fair child and large of his age."

On this occasion no reference appears to have been made to the treasure that West was carrying back with him to England ; but in a letter to her brother, dated April 11th, Margaret returned to the charge.

" We cannot believe," she wrote, after returning thanks to him for his loving letters, delivered to her by Dr. West, " that, of your mind or by your command we are so freindly [*sic*] dealt with in our father's legacy : whereof we would not have spoken, nor written, had not the doctor now spoken to us of the same in his credence. Our husband knows that it is withholden for his sake and will recompense us so far as the doctor show him. We are ashamed therewith, and would God never word had been thereof : it is not worth such estimation as is in your divers letters of the same. And we lack nothing ; our husband is ever the longer the better to us, as knows God."

Yet Margaret would have liked to have had her rights, and by this time she must have been convinced that she was not destined to get them.

CHAPTER XVI

1513

Preparations for war—James's attempt at conciliation—
Bishop Forman at Paris—His equivocal character—
Scotland and the Council partisans of France—Henry
crosses the Channel—Scottish fleet despatched to France
—Anne of Brittany's " love-letter " to James—Arran's
failure to execute his orders.

FROM the ill success of Dr. West's mission
Henry will no doubt have formed his conclusions, and will have inferred that his brother-in-
law was not to be prevented from fulfilling his
promises to France, even should such fulfilment involve the breach of his engagements to
England. It therefore behoved both parties
to make ready for the consequences.

The English envoy had paid a visit to Leith
—" for a pastime," to quote his own account
of the expedition. He may, however, have
had a more serious purpose than he professed.
He had certainly carefully inspected the shipping
there, and the naval operations that were in

progress, and though he belittled what he had seen, his observations were fully reported. He had then proceeded to Newhaven, where James had erected a dock for the purpose of ship-building, and had raised a chapel for the use of the many workmen employed at the arsenal.

If James was busy, Henry was not less so, and had taken measures without delay to prepare for the contingency of a Scottish invasion. The Earl of Surrey had been dispatched to Yorkshire to enlist an army and to hold it in readiness, should occasion arise for making use of it. But though Surrey executed his orders and placed garrisons in such towns as he considered required them, all appeared to be quiet on the Border, and he returned to London.

So far, no step had been taken to put an end to the nominal terms of peace between the two Kings, nor had anything occurred which could be construed as a definite breach of the treaty. Towards the end of May, a letter was written by James with an ostensible purpose of a distinctly pacific nature; since it demanded a safe-conduct for the indefatigable Forman, in order that he might visit London with the object of arranging a " universal peace."

The document was couched in language of the utmost courtesy and the King displayed a desire for the advice of his young brother-in-law. His main motive, however, was not one to commend itself to a man smarting under a recent failure and eager to retrieve and avenge it.

"Our brother, the most Christian King of France," wrote James, "has lately written to us that he and the Catholic King of Aragon have taken, the first day of April past, truce to endure for one whole year . . . as we doubt not ye are informed. . . . Whereupon our brother of France has desired us to enter into the same truce if you enter into the same. Wherefore we have sent to you as well to have knowledge if you enter into this truce or not, as to have your advice what you think we should do for our part. Praying you, if you accept the same, to advertise us hastily, that we may help to treat for amity and peace as we have been ever ready to do. . . ." The letter goes on to condole, in characteristic fashion, for the death of one of the Howards, whose loss to his master, as a distinguished sailor, James was peculiarly ready to recognise :

" Surely, dearest brother, we think more loss

is to you of your late admiral, who deceased to his great honour and laud, than the advantage might have been of the winning of all the French galleys and their equipages. The said valiant Knight's service and other noblemen that on both sides apparently be perished, were better applied upon the enemies of Christ whereon all Christian men were well at war." After which he repeated the expression of his sorrow at the Admiral's death, the more so that he was the son of the Earl of Surrey, "that noble Knight who conveyed our dearest fellow the Queen to us."

Nothing came of this last overture of peace, if it was intended to be such. James must have known that there was little chance that, at this stage in the affair, his brother-in-law would draw back; and though, owing to West's endeavours, a meeting of English and Scottish commissioners had been arranged to take place in June, the conference produced no good result. The English members of it would have liked to postpone a decision till October—a delay which would have met with their master's full approval.

Bishop Forman was at the French court, having reached it by sea, since Henry had re-

fused the proposed messenger of peace a
safe-conduct through England ; and again the
equivocal nature of the envoy's dealings makes
itself felt. Two years later a charge was
preferred against him by the Scottish authorities, who told the Pope that he had incited his
master to make war with England, a fact
which would explain his appointment to the
French Archbishopric of Bourges. Yet in treating with Henry VII he had permitted the title
of King of France to be included in those assumed by the English sovereign, bringing some
trouble on his own master by his conduct in
this respect. He had the gift of acquiring
friends wherever he went ; and the see of St.
Andrews was shortly bestowed upon him by the
new Pope, Leo X.

At home and abroad, by his subjects and by
others, James was being skilfully entangled in
the net destined to prove his destruction. Ireland lent her aid towards fanning the flame,
and O'Donnell crossed the channel to offer
his homage to the King of Scots, and to do what
in him lay to excite him further against his
personal foe, Henry. De la Motte, the French
ambassador, paid another visit to Edinburgh,
bringing four ships, laden with flour and wine

and golden coin, together with prizes captured from the English, to solicit James's aid in the approaching struggle. And beyond and besides all this, there was the general feeling of the nation. West had not been mistaken when he described it as vehement in French partisanship.

French partisanship and, doubtless, antagonism towards England. At a later date and when the matter had been brought to a practical issue, it was true that caution got the better of both, and that many of the nobles would have drawn back and moved the King from his purpose. At this time, not only popular sentiment and passion were in favour of war—as is generally the case—but a majority of the Council concurred in the view. The French envoy received a royal welcome, and at a meeting of the Council, called together to consider his demand for support, many of its members were of opinion that, should it be found impossible to deter Henry from making an attack upon France, war should forthwith be declared. Another and more prudent section of the Council, led by Elphinstone, Bishop of Aberdeen, demurred. Henry was young; he was wealthy, and his people, enriched by the

long peace, and weary of inaction, were eager
for war. The preparations he had made for
hostilities with France would be turned against
Scotland, and Scotland had sustained no injuries at the hands of the English sufficient to
justify her in taking up arms. An embassy
should therefore be sent to dissuade Henry
from carrying out his purpose, and his answer
should be awaited before any action was taken,
the results of unsuccess being apparently left
vague.

The discussion was carried on with unusual
violence ; order was preserved with difficulty,
and Elphinstone was said to have spoken like
a crazy old man against the public interest and
the ancient pledge binding Scotland to France.
The King's inclinations were towards war, and
the party advocating it triumphed.

In any case it must have been felt by this time
that a policy which included amongst its chances
that of turning Henry from his settled determination was doomed to failure. By June 30th
any lingering hopes entertained on the subject
had been extinguished. Henry had taken the
decisive step of crossing the Channel, and had
placed himself in person at the head of his
troops.

James's response was prompt. His fleet was at once made ready to go to sea, and by July 27th it was prepared to set sail. On the previous day the Lyon Herald had been dispatched to France, with orders to seek Henry in his camp and to carry what was virtually a declaration of war.

The fleet which thus set forth consisted of some twenty vessels. The King's cousin, the Earl of Arran—the same who had been detained in custody by Henry—was in command, and the King himself, on board his great *St. Michael*, accompanied the fleet as far as the island of May. It was no fault of James's that the ships and the three thousand men they carried were to prove of no avail in the cause of the French. His orders had been clear ; they were not carried out. Whether in wilful disobedience or through misapprehension or incompetence, Arran wholly failed to execute the King's commands, and instead of making for France " passed upon the west seas on the coast of Ireland . . . there landed and burnt Carrickfergus, with all other villages, and then came to the town of Ayr and there landed and played themselves and reposed for the space of forty days." [1]

[1] Lindsay of Pitscottie.

When the anticipated support from James did not arrive, indignation was felt on the other side of the water. Forman, at the French court, was hot for war. The Bishop of Durham —one Ruthal—stated in a letter to Wolsey written after the battle of Flodden, on the authority of Sir William Scot, James's Chancellor, one of the few prisoners taken alive, that the Bishop of Moray had instigated the King's sensual mind to make war, contrary to the minds of all the nobles of Scotland, " insomuch as he supposed the said Bishop will never come into Scotland, for if he do he is in danger. He saith also that in the said Bishop there is neither wisdom, learning, nor virtue, but lying, dissimulation, bribery, and all untruth." The verdict was pronounced when the war promoted by Forman had proved disastrous, but there was probably a measure of truth in it. It is said that he took upon himself to write " very sharply " to his master, telling him that his honour would be the forfeit if he did not keep the promises made by his envoy in his name. Louis's Queen, Anne of Brittany, for her part made an emotional appeal to the spirit of chivalry and romance known to be so marked a feature of James's character. According to

16

Lindsay, she wrote him a love-letter, "naming him her love, showing him that she had suffered much rebuke for his sake in France, for the defending of his honour ; wherefore she believed he would recompense her with some of his knightly support in such a necessity—that is, that he would raise an army, and come three feet on English ground for her sake, and to that effect she sent him a ring off her finger."

What share the Queen's intervention had in strengthening James's purpose must be matter of conjecture. All the means taken to urge upon him war with England were only to spur a willing horse. Accumulated grievances upon the Border, with the growing rivalry upon the seas and the naval conflicts that had already taken place, had combined to give rise to a condition of irritation liable at any moment to produce an outbreak, even had the present attack upon Scotland's old ally, France, not afforded a more substantial cause of quarrel.

The upbraiding letters from Paris brought the first news of Arran's failure to execute his orders ; and when James shortly afterwards learnt that the fleet he had believed to be off the coast of France was at no greater distance than Ayr, his indignation was great, and Sir Andrew Wood was sent forthwith to assume the command. According to one authority[1] the earl added to his delinquencies by a refusal to relinquish his post : " This lord, being young, notwithstanding he heard the terrible message of the King, yet he would not give over his office at the King's command, but pulled up sails and passed wherever he pleased, thinking that he would come to France in due time."

Thus ended James's first definitely warlike move. The sequel, so far as the fleet is concerned, is veiled in obscurity. That a landing in France was effected by Arran with the troops entrusted to him appears to be proved by the pension afterwards settled upon him for life by Louis. But there is no record of any exploits performed by him and his Scots, unless it is to be inferred that they took their part in the fight known as the Battle of the Spurs.

The ultimate fate of the fleet, of the vessels over the building of which James had watched so anxiously and expended so much thought and care, is an example of the powerlessness

[1] Pitscottie. Pinkerton concludes that Arran had sailed before James's mandate reached him.

of a man to shape the course of even the near future, or to further the causes he has most at heart. Some of the ships that had sailed for France returned, we are told, to Scotland, where, their master dead, they mouldered in neglect; some of them were sold to France; and the great *St. Michael*, which had cost so much labour and expense, was purchased by Louis XII, not much more than six months after the King's death, from the Scottish Government with the Duke of Albany at its head.[1]

[1] Pinkerton.

CHAPTER XVII

1513

Lyon King-at-Arms at Henry's camp—Henry's reply— The " Ill Raid "—Scotland called to arms—Signs and omens—King and Queen part.

IT will be remembered that, the day before the fleet had sailed, as James intended, for France, Lyon King-at-Arms had been dispatched to seek Henry. His mission was faithfully executed. He found the King encamped before Terouenne with the Emperor Maximilian, who had joined him with a small body of troops and had shown himself content to serve under the English flag and to wear the cross of St. George.

The interview between the Scottish herald and the English King has been fully reported by the various chroniclers.[1]

Brought into the presence of the young King —Henry was still no more than twenty-two—the Scot, though represented as having been some-

[1] Hall, Holinshed, etc.

what dismayed at finding him so nobly accompanied, proceeded to deliver, " with few words and meet reverence," the missive with which he had been entrusted.

The document was a long one, and set forth in the first place James's manifold causes of complaint, enumerating the wrongs he had sustained without redress at Henry's hands. Heron and his accomplices in murder had found protection in England ; Margaret's legacy had been withheld ; Andrew Barton had been slaughtered, and his ships and artillery retained. Having recapitulated his personal injuries, James passed on to Henry's present action towards the King of France, " whom you have caused to lose his country of Milan, and now invade him, who is with us in second degree of blood, and has been unto you kind without offence, and more kinder than to us. Notwithstanding, in defence of his person we must take part." To James Henry had been neither just nor kind, " proceeding always to the utter destruction of our nearest friends," and going so far as to refuse a safe-conduct to the messengers whom, by Dr. West's desire, he would have sent to confer with him and to endeavour to make peace between England

and France—a thing unheard of even amongst infidels. "Therefore we write to you this time at length plainness of our mind, that we require and desire you to desist from further invasion and utter destruction of our brother and cousin, the most Christian King, to whom . . . we are bounden and obliged for mutual defence . . . certifying you we will take part in [his] defence."

The King received the letter from Lyon's hands and read it. In the answer he made to the herald fierce anger mingled with bitter reproach. He now saw—so he said—that the King of Scotland was that which he had ever believed him to be. He had never esteemed him to be of any truth, and so it proved, since he was breaking his oath and invading England in Henry's absence, which he dared not have done had he been at home. By this he showed himself "not to be degenerate from the condition of his forefathers, whose faiths for the most part hath ever been violated and their promises never observed farther than they list." Never again would James be included in any league to which Henry was a party. There was an earl left in England, however, able to oppose him and all his power, so that the country would not be found destitute, as he believed.

"But thus say to thy master, that I am the very owner of Scotland, and that he holdeth it of me by homage ; and inasmuch as now he doth rebel against me, with God's help I shall at my return expulse him from his realm, and so tell him."

Lyon King-at-Arms refused boldly to be the bearer of any message of the kind. He would take no such words of reproach to his King, but only any letters that Henry might send.

"'Then,' said the King, 'wherefore came you hither? Will you receive no answer?'

"'Yes,' said Lyon, 'your answer requireth doing and no writing ; that is, that immediately you should return home.'

"'Well,' said the King, 'I will return to your damage at my pleasure and not at thy master's summoning.'"

The letter that was in the end entrusted to Lyon was conceived in the same spirit as the verbal message the herald had declined to take. Passing over with contemptuous brevity James's recapitulation of his wrongs—to every one of which Henry asserted that a reasonable answer,

founded upon law and conscience, had already
been returned—he repeated that he could not
marvel at the intention the King declared of
taking part with Louis against him, since it
was in accordance with the ancient accustomed
manners of James's progenitors, "who never
kept longer faith and promise than pleased
them." Had James been bound by love and
dread of God, by nearness of blood, honour of
the world, or law and reason, he would never
thus have acted, especially in Henry's absence ;
and the Pope and all christened princes might
note his dishonourable behaviour. Only now,
when Henry was at a distance, had he uttered
the old rancour of his mind, so long kept secret.
Nevertheless, remembering the brittleness of his
promise, and suspecting, though not wholly
believing, so much unsteadfastness, Henry had
not left his realm unprepared for resistance.

Such was the letter committed, on August
12th, to the herald. Being delayed by the
difficulty of obtaining a passage, it was not
until after the fatal battle had been fought that
the bearer reached Scotland, when the man to
whom it was addressed was already dead. Had
things fallen out otherwise, it would have made
little difference. Reproaches, upbraiding, anger

—the time was gone by when these could have taken effect upon James. He was bent upon war, and it is likely enough that if, by some unlooked-for chance, Henry had composed his quarrel with the French King and had left him no excuse for drawing the sword, it would have been a disappointment rather than the reverse. His old love of fighting had re-awakened and he was eager to begin the combat—

> When on, as to his sport, he sped—
> His stake a life, a crown;
> And radiant, hence to ruin led
> The world's best manhood down." [1]

By some of his subjects his zeal was outrun. Lord Home, Warden of the Marches, had collected some three or four thousand men, and made a raid—the " Ill Raid," as it came to be called, when it had proved unsuccessful—across the Border, burning and pillaging the villages that lay in his path. Whether the foray was hazarded on Home's private responsibility or whether James had authorised it, seems uncertain. In either case the unwisdom of the venture is manifest. The northern English counties were prepared for resistance; the

[1] *On Flodden Edge*, Sir George Douglas.

success of so small a force as that led by
Home must have been more than doubtful,
and the expedition would serve as an intimation to England that hostilities were to be
expected and set her on her guard. In point
of fact, it resulted in defeat. As the body
of marauders were making their way back,
laden with booty, to Scotland, a thousand
Englishmen, waiting in ambush, fell upon them,
put them to flight and recaptured the spoil.
The preliminary round had ended ill for the
Scots.

James meanwhile had issued a summons,
bidding the entire military array of the kingdom
to meet him in the third week of August at
the Borough Muir, near Edinburgh—" a field
then spacious and delightful by the shades
of many stately and aged oaks." [1] The usual
provisions, to last for forty days, were to be
brought. Should the army be kept together
after that length of time—an unprecedented
contingency—it would be at the sovereign's cost.

The response made to the summons is proof
of the ascendancy that James had obtained
over his people ; and it is calculated that
100,000 men rallied to arms in obedience to

[1] Drummond.

his behest.[1] " This proclamation," says Lindsay, " was hastily obeyed, contrary to the Council of Scotland's will. Yet nevertheless they both loved and feared him so that they would not refuse him."

If the Council had had time to reconsider their decision since the day that they had been so hot in their desire to take up arms in the cause of France, it was now too late for repentance ; and the consciousness of their change of attitude would only have availed to deprive the King of the support afforded by the consciousness of sympathy and approval. Tidings of Home's discomfiture had also by this time reached Edinburgh and may have contributed to alter his mood. Afterwards, in the face of the enemy, his spirits revived and the old game of war regained its attraction. But when he appeared at the Council-board at Linlithgow it was noted that he was " very sad and dolorous."

There may have been other causes for his dejection. What he felt at this juncture can

---

[1] Colonel Elliot considers it impossible that all the forces met near Edinburgh, pointing out the folly that would have been involved in bringing the borderers in especial so far north.—*The Field of Flodden*, Hon. F. Elliot.

JAMES IV, KING OF SCOTLAND.
From a painting by Holbein.

be no more than matter of conjecture, but that
it was a time of deep anxiety cannot be doubted.
He had deliberately chosen his course ; he was
committed to it by act and word, and would
have found it difficult, almost indeed impossible,
to draw back.   His defiance had been sent to
Henry, he was pledged to the French King,
his nation was under arms—all was in prepara-
tion for the fight.   And yet, at the eleventh
hour, doubts may have assailed him and a
reaction may have set in.   James was a man
of a brooding mind and given to scruples.   He
held his honour dear, and for honour's sake
and for the sake of the league binding him to
France he was flinging himself into the fray.
But the question may have forced itself upon
him whether there was no other bond that he
was breaking.   What of the " perpetual peace "
he had sworn to the Tudors ?—the Tudors
from whom as a token of reconciliation and
amity he had received the wife whose blood
ran in the veins of his little son.   Now that
no English envoy was at hand to rouse antagonism, the point so often and urgently
raised may have pressed with the greater
force, and he may have asked himself whether,
in truth, in keeping one pledge there had been

no violation of another, and that other a pledge the breach of which, by the terms of the treaty of 1502, involved the penalty of excommunication. Such questions might well harass and perplex him, and oppress him with an intolerable weight of responsibility, all the greater because he found himself standing alone, dissociated from the opinion of the lords of his Council.

Signs and wonders followed, admirably calculated further to dash his spirits. Whilst he was at Linlithgow, a singular scene took place. Vespers were being sung, in the presence of King and court, when an old and venerable man was seen to enter, bareheaded, the Cathedral, his bright gold hair, thin on his head, falling to his shoulders, and wearing a long blue robe, bound by a linen girdle.

Coming swiftly forward he cried out that he desired to speak with the King, and leaning over the desk where James knelt in prayer, with no reverence or salutation, he delivered his message.

"Sir King," he said, "my mother has sent me to thee, desiring thee not to go where thou art purposed; which, if thou do, thou shalt not fare well in thy journey, nor none that is with thee. Further, she forbad thee not to

LINLITHGOW PALACE.
Photo by Francis C. Inglis.

254]

mingle nor use the counsel of women ; which
if thou do, thou wilt be confounded and brought
to shame."

" When this man had spoken these words to
the King, the evensong was near done, and the
King paused on these words, studying to give
him an answer."

Before he could do so, under his eyes and in
the presence of all the surrounding Lords, the
stranger vanished out of sight, and though Sir
David Lindsay, then a young man, and others
of the King's servants sought to seize him, they
could not. Nor was anything further heard of
him, though a tradition lingered in the place
that he had afterwards been seen crossing the
court towards the palace.

Margaret has very commonly been credited
with having had a hand in arranging a scene
skilfully adapted to take effect upon her husband's sensitive mind, and the warning against
women gives colour to the surmise. It is
certain that she would have done her best to
obviate war with her native land. She had also
conceived a somewhat irrational jealousy of
Anne of Brittany—irrespective of the fact that
she and James had never met—demanding of
him why he preferred to please the Queen of

France rather than herself, his wife and the mother of his children, and further stigmatising Anne as " twice married, by means of divorces."

It appears, besides, that though in no wise addicted to superstitious fancies or fears, she was at this special time troubled, on her own showing, by strange dreams containing premonitions of disaster, which she recounted to the King in the evident hope of turning him from his purpose. She had seen James himself, in a vision, hurled down a precipice and crushed below it ; and diamonds had been transmuted as she gazed at them into pearls, symbols of widowhood and tears.

Dreams, apparitions, entreaties, the disapprobation of serious advisers, proved alike ineffectual. Ineffectual likewise were Margaret's representations that the one little child who, should his father fall, would alone be left to wear the crown, was too weak a defence against the enemies of the Scottish nation. Though the King's mind might be overshadowed by forebodings as the result of all that had been done to produce them, no arguments could induce him to abandon the enterprise he had undertaken. His doom was fixed.

Leaving Linlithgow, he hastened back to

Edinburgh, there to complete his military preparations and to bring forth the artillery and cannon that were to accompany the army on its expedition.

Whilst this work was being carried forward a fresh marvel took place. " A cry was heard at the market Cross of Edinburgh at the hour of midnight proclaiming as it had been a summons, which was named and called by the proclaimer thereof, The Summons of Plotcock (*i.e.* some fiend) ; which desired all men ' To compear, both Earl and Lord, and Baron and Gentleman, and all honest gentlemen within the town (every man being specified by his own name), within the space of forty days, before his master, where it should happen him to appoint, and be for the time, under the pain of disobedience.' But whether," continues the chronicler impartially, " this summons was proclaimed by vain persons, night-walkers, or drunk men, for their pastime, or if it was but a spirit, I cannot truly tell : But it was shown to me that an in-dweller of the town, Mr. Richard Lawson, being evil disposed, ganging in his gallery-stair foranent the Cross, hearing this voice proclaiming this summons, thought marvel what it should be, cried on his servant

17

to bring him his purse, and when he had brought him it, he took out a crown and cast over the stair, saying, ' I appeal from that summons, judgment and sentence thereof, and stakes me all whole in the mercy of God, Christ Jesus his Son.' ''

The authority quoted by Lindsay of Pitscottie, who tells the story, was a gentleman, then twenty years old, who had been in Edinburgh when the incident occurred ; '' and thereafter, when the field was stricken, he swore to me there was no man that escaped that was called in this summons, but that one man alone which made his protestation and appealed from the said summons ; but all the lave were perished in the field with the King.''

The next morning news of what had happened spread through the city, till it reached the King's ears. What he thought of it is not told. Neither does it appear whether his name had headed the fatal list, or whether fiend or trickster had flinched from including the chief victim in the sentence pronounced against subordinates. What is certain is that neither did this ominous scene, any more than all that had preceded it, avail to turn him from his determination.

His preparations were complete. Earlier in the month he had made his last pilgrimage to the shrine of St. Duthac ; there perhaps to appeal to a higher court from the sentence of excommunication pronounced upon him. For James was to die excommunicate, not by reason of his sins, which were many, but because Henry was in favour with Rome, and a mistaken chivalry, strengthened by an old grudge, had armed his brother-in-law against him. Was the sentence just ? Technically there can be no doubt that, by the terms of the treaty with England, which treaty he had determined to break, he had incurred it. For the rest, " an unjust excommunication," wrote John Major, weighing the question five years later, " is no more an excommunication than a dead man is a man. No one, unless by reason of some mortal sin, should be excommunicated . . . wherefore I think that many who are excommunicated are in grace. Neither will a false sentence hurt a man in his spiritual life, whether he be buried in consecrated or unconsecrated ground ; nor will every man who dies under a censure justly pronounced, be damned, if he have sufficiently laboured for his absolution." [1]

[1] Major, *The Days of James IV.*, Gregory Smith.

His pilgrimage made, his preparations ended, it remained for James to take leave of his wife. Margaret would have liked to accompany him south. A rumour had reached her that her brother's wife, Queen Katharine, would be with the English troops, and she appears to have hoped that, between them, peace might yet have been made. But she did not obtain her desire. The King took leave of her in friendly fashion, confiding to her, she afterwards said, where his treasure was placed, " in case that aught happened other than good to him." He also handed over to her, in trust for his little son, the last consignment of money he had received from France, with much other valuable property. To Elphinstone, Bishop of Aberdeen, who had so strenuously opposed his war policy and who has been described as his good genius, James entrusted the keeping of his will and the care of his heir. Margaret was made the child's tutrix, in case of the King's death, so long as she remained unmarried.

Thus husband and wife parted for the last time. By August 22nd James had crossed the Tweed, and with forces variously estimated at from 60,000 to 100,000 men, had reached Twizel, where a council was held two days later, and it was enacted that the heirs of all who might be slain in the coming campaign should be exempted from the usual royal dues of wardship, relief, and marriage. These arrangements, no less than those made before leaving Edinburgh, point to the fact that the King was fully alive to the gravity of the situation and the risks incurred. The war with England had begun.

CHAPTER XVIII

1513

The Border crossed—Norham Castle captured—Lady Heron
—Surrey's challenge accepted by James—Angus's
protest—The Scots on Flodden Hill—Movements of the
English forces.

ON August 26th, four days after James had
crossed the Border, Surrey, in chief command
of the English forces, started northwards from
York. Hearing of the King's intention to lay
siege to Norham, he had sent to inquire from the
captain in charge there whether the castle
was in danger, in which case he would come to
defend it. The answer had been reassuring.
The captain returned thanks to the earl for his
offer ; but he " prayed God that the King of
Scots would come with his puissance, for he
would keep him play till the time that the King
of England came out of France to rescue it,
which answer rejoiced the earl much." At
Durham, having marched thither on "the foulest
day and night that could be, and the ways so

deep insomuch that his guide was almost drowned before him," Surrey was met by tidings of what had come of the boast. "The King of Scots with his great ordnance had rased the walls of the castle of Norham, and had made three great assaults three days together, and the captain valiantly defended him, but he spent vainly so much of his ordnance, bows and arrows and other munitions, that at the last he tacked, and so was at the sixth day compelled to yield him simply to the King's mercy. This castle was thought impregnable, if it had been well furnished, but the Scots, by the undiscreet spending of the captain, took it in six days. This chance was more sorrowful to the earl than to the bishop, owner of the same." [1]

It was indeed bad news. As Surrey paused at Durham it seemed that worse might follow; for the wind was blowing a tempest; his son, Thomas Howard, Lord Admiral, was expected to arrive from France; and, listening to the blast, his father was beset by fears lest he might perish at sea.

If Thomas Ruthal, Bishop of Durham, is to be trusted, the satisfaction of the Scots at their initial success was clouded by scruples. Norham

[1] Hall.

was apparently supposed to be under the special protection of St. Cuthbert, whose banner had been lent to the English army, and in a letter written after the battle of Flodden to Wolsey, containing many questionable statements, Ruthal mentions a report to the effect that " after the King of Scots meddled with Norham 20,000 of his men went away from him, thinking verily that a mischief would follow upon that act, wishing they had never meddled with the said castle."

It may be doubted whether regard for an English saint, whose banner was carried in the ranks of the enemy, would have affected the consciences of their antagonists; and in his account of the subsequent battle, the Bishop himself describes how, the whole retinue of the bishopric with St. Cuthbert's banner having joined in the fight, " the Scots had most disrespect to the said banner, and set most fiercely upon it."

However that might be, the capture of Norham was an encouraging beginning to the war; and it was followed by a series of further successes. Dividing his forces into two divisions, James, in command of one of them, marched south, by the right bank of the river Till, to

Etal, and after seizing and destroying its castle, made himself likewise master of Ford Castle, a mile higher up the river, thus obtaining possession of the only two bridges except Twizel, near the Tweed, and Weetwood, ten miles farther south, by which the Till could be crossed. Whilst James was thus occupied, the second division of his army, crossing the river at Twizel, had taken and destroyed the castle of Wark, rejoining the King when this had been accomplished.

The capture of Ford was attended, if certain chroniclers are to be believed, by serious consequences. The castle belonged to Heron, brother of the man concerned in the murder of Ker. In default of the true culprit, he was at present detained in confinement in Scotland ; but his wife, with her daughter, was at home, and it is said that James, falling a victim to the attraction of the older woman, lingered on, wasting precious days at Ford when wisdom and generalship demanded that he should make the most of his time, and strike a decisive blow at Berwick, ill prepared at the moment for defence. It is also reported that his son, Erasmus's pupil, the young Archbishop of St. Andrews, who ac-

companied the expedition, was in love with
Lady Heron's daughter, "against the order
of all good captains of war, before any good
success of battle and victory." [1]

Lord Surrey was meanwhile marching north
at the head of some 26,000 men. At Durham
he had been joined by Lord Dacre, Sir W.
Bulmer, Sir Marmaduke Constable and others,
whom he appointed to meet him at Bolton on
September 4th. Delayed by the weather at
Alnwick, he was there relieved from his anxiety
on account of his son, who arrived at the head
of a welcome contingent of disciplined soldiers
detached by Henry from his camp in France.

James was still at Ford, where the enterprise which had been opened with success
was beginning to assume a less hopeful aspect.
Brief campaigns were the custom of the
day; already the provisions brought by the
army were running short, and when the in-
clemency of the weather is likewise taken into
account—not one fair day had interrupted

---

[1] Pitscottie. Doubt has been thrown upon the whole of
the episode connected with Lady Heron, for which the
authorities are Buchanan and Pitscottie. The accounts of
the chroniclers must of course be accepted with caution, but
it cannot be denied that James's character and past give a
probability to the story it might otherwise have lacked.

the long spell of " great cold, wind, and wet "
since the Border had been crossed—it is not
surprising that the undisciplined forces commanded by James should have begun to dis-
perse, some directing their steps northward
with the intention of procuring fresh provisions
and returning to their duty, others doubtless
glad of an excuse to remain no longer in the
field. Yet, in spite of the dwindling of his
forces, James, " as a man uncounsellable,"
seemed to feel no fear.

What followed next rests on authority that
has been disputed. It is said that Lady
Heron proved eminently successful in turning
the hold she had obtained over the King to
the advantage of her countrymen—that in a
position to form a just opinion of the condition
of the invading forces ; perceiving that their
numbers were largely diminished and that
provisions were scanty ; in possession also of
the King's secrets and intentions, and probably
not unaware that the wiser of his followers were
bringing pressure to bear to induce him to rest
satisfied with the successes he had achieved
and to return to Scotland, she proposed to go
southward and to effect a meeting with certain
of her friends ; after which she would return

to Ford and bring the King tidings of all that was going forward amongst the English.

It would seem that even a man in love would have hesitated to trust a woman ready, on her own showing, to betray her countrymen. But with almost incredible folly James, placing full confidence in her good faith, is said to have consented to her suggestion, and even to have sent an escort with her part of her way. Which done, he waited in vain at Ford for her return, and "never knew the coming of the Englishmen till their whole armies were within the space of three Scottish miles to him.[1] . . . When the news was shown to the King of Scotland he would scarcely believe them, but leapt upon horse and rode to the head of a hill to see."

Lady Heron had in fact at once proceeded to the English camp, had furnished Surrey with all the information in her power, and had advised an immediate attack upon James whilst his force was weak and supplies scanty.

Such is the story told by the chronicler, to be taken for what it is worth. What is certain is that Surrey, reinforced by the contingent brought from France, aware of the enemy's

[1] Pitscottie. A manifest mis-statement.

failing strength, and possibly fearing that
James might yield to wiser counsels and turn
his steps homewards without giving battle,
showed his comprehension of the man with
whom he had to do by sending him from
Alnwick on Sunday, September 4th, a challenge
to meet him in battle on a given day—the
following Friday, September 9th, being that
named. To his father's challenge Lord Thomas
Howard added an insolent message of his own.
He had, he said, sought the Scottish navy on
the sea but could not meet with it, because it
was fled to France by the Irish coast. James
had often caused him to be called to account
to make redress for Andrew Barton, a pirate,
whom he had long before vanquished. Howard
was now come, in his proper person, to justify
Andrew's death in the vanguard of the field
and would see what could be laid to his charge.
A menace followed. Neither he nor his company would take any Scottish noble prisoner,
nor any other—they should die if they came in
danger from him, unless it were the King himself, for he trusted to none other courtesy at
the hands of the Scots.[1]

It was clearly the intention of father and son

[1] Hall.

to force an instant battle. Rouge Croix, the English herald, carried Surrey's challenge, and added the defiance of his son. More cautious than James, the earl, lest the Scottish herald who brought back the answer should act as a spy on the movements and arrangement of the English army, met James's messenger in the early morning of Tuesday, September 6th, at some distance from his camp and there heard the reply that the King had made.

In response to the earl's proposal that the fight should take place on the Friday, " the King his master bade him show to the earl that he was as welcome as any nobleman in England to the same King, and that if he had been at home at his town of Edinburgh, there receiving such a message from the said earl, he would gladly have come and fulfilled the said earl's desire, and the said herald assured the earl on the King his master's behalf that the said King would abide him in battle at the day prefixed." [1]

Surrey had obtained what he wanted—had successfully traded upon the qualities which made James the knight-errant rather than the general—and was right joyous, giving much praise to the honourable agreement of the

[1] Hall.

King. The Scottish Council were less content and met together, it would seem privately, to consult as to how James could be prevented from fighting at a disadvantage.

As they discussed the situation, they were not aware that they had the King himself for a listener.[1] Unrecognised, he had repaired to the place where the meeting was held and heard all that went on. It was little to his liking. Patrick, Lord Lindsay, as the oldest member of the Council, was first called upon to speak; and gave it as his opinion that for James to meet Surrey in combat would be as if a merchant was to risk a rose noble against the halfpenny stake of a common gambler. Were he to win, he would be little the gainer; were he to lose, with the gold honour would also be lost. Scotland was the player, the King the rose noble which would be ventured, and England the common gambler, who only hazarded a halfpenny—namely " an old crooked carle in a chariot." [2] The King should therefore be removed out of danger, whilst those of his lords he judged best fitted should risk themselves for his pleasure, their own honour, and the welfare of the country.

[1] Lindsay of Pitscottie.   [2] Surrey was nearly seventy.

Lindsay's conclusion found favour with all present, and they went so far as to name the nobles who should lead the battle, the King from a distance, with others of his lords, acting as spectators of the fight.

It seems strange, if the story is founded on fact, that the men who knew James so well could have believed that the part they assigned him was one he would consent to play. Having listened to what was said, he broke into the conference with an outburst of anger and indignation. He would fight with England that day, though all of them should swear the contrary. Though they might leave him and fly, they should not put him to shame according to their device, and as for Patrick Lindsay, who had been the first to give his vote in favour of it, " I vow to God I shall never see Scotland sooner nor I shall cause hang him over his own yett."

The King prevailed, nor could the Council, " seeing him in a fury," resist his will. Yet the Earl of Angus still pleaded with him.[1] Great in years and authority, he laboured to turn James from his purpose. His duty by the King of France had been performed ; forces

[1] Holinshed and Buchanan.

had been diverted from Henry's invading army.
The English troops could now neither injure
France nor could they remain long in the
north, in a cold and barren country, where
there was no corn and winter was coming on
apace. If the French ambassador urged the
King to fight—as he had been doing—he was
a foreigner, nor was it to be wondered at that
he should be over lavish in pouring out the
blood of other men. The Scots were few in
number, but they included all who excelled in
force, authority, or counsel. Were they to be
slain, the kingdom would speedily fall a prey.

But neither would James listen to Angus, only
commanding him, in heat, to go home, if he
feared the enemy. The old man burst into
tears.

"If my past life does not free me from any
suspicion of cowardice," he said, "I know not
what can." As long as he was capable of
exertion he had never spared it for the safety
of the country or the honour of his King. Now
his advice was all that he had to give, and it
being despised, departing, he left behind his
two sons, his friends and his kin, "And I
pray God that He make this fear of mine to
be false, and that I may rather be counted a

18

lying prophet than behold those things which I fear will happen unto us."

So Angus took his departure and went home, leaving the King to his fate. At the battle which followed both his sons, with two hundred others of his name, were slain.

Meantime Rouge Croix, returning to the English camp, had brought with him the news that the Scottish forces were no longer where he had found them at Ford, but occupied a position which might have gone far to counterbalance weakness in numbers. On Tuesday, the 6th, or even earlier, the bridge at Ford had been crossed, and joining the contingent on the left bank of the Till, James lay on the side of the steep hill of Flodden facing southward in the direction from which the enemy might be expected to arrive. At the foot of the slope the Scottish ordnance was massed, and on one side a marsh or bog afforded additional protection to the invading force.

This was the intelligence that met Surrey when—on the same Tuesday that James's move was made—he reached Woolerhaugh, six miles distant from Flodden Hill, and there halted. It was evident that to attack the Scots from below would be to fight at

extreme disadvantage, nor was Surrey disposed
to hazard it. On the afternoon of Wednesday,
the 7th, he dispatched Rouge Croix once more
to seek James in his camp, the bearer of a
letter in which he attempted again to play
upon the King's rash courage. Protesting
against the removal of the Scots from Ford,
whither his challenge had been sent, to a
position " more like a fortress or camp " than
the " indifferent ground " which would furnish
a fair field, he boldly suggested that the King
should descend to Milfield plain on the morrow,
where he would meet him between twelve and
three in the afternoon.[1]

On this occasion James refused to be fooled.
Surrey had gone too far; the herald was not
admitted to his presence; and when the
message was transmitted through a servant,
the King replied that it did not beseem an
earl so to handle a King, that he would use
no sorcery, nor did he trust in any ground.
He would take and keep his own ground at
his own pleasure, and not at the assigning of
the Earl of Surrey.

Having failed in his endeavour to dislodge
the Scots from their vantage ground, a change

[1] *Calendar of State Papers.*

of tactics on the part of their adversaries was clearly necessary. Surrey was not a man to risk all on so doubtful a venture as an attack upon Flodden Hill from the lower ground lying to the south of it ; and on September 8th he took the step of crossing the Till by Weetwood bridge and encamped two miles north-west of Barmoor Castle.

The advantages of the move have been pointed out by a military expert.[1] By this means Surrey exchanged a long line of communications with Newcastle for a short one with Berwick. He was also afforded the option either of effecting an invasion of Scotland without an encounter with the Scottish troops, all on the opposite side of the Till, or of remaining where he was, whilst James's forces would suffer increasingly from want of supplies and the other inconveniences attending a sojourn in a hostile country. "In my opinion," concludes Colonel Elliot, " by the evening of the 8th Surrey had already gained the campaign," adding that had the English commander elected to remain stationary until the Scots had been compelled by circumstances to beat a retreat, the result

[1] Lieut.-Col. the Hon. Fitzwilliam Elliot, to whose book on the Battle of Flodden I am largely indebted.

would have been in his belief even more disastrous to Scotland than the battle which was to take place.

On this evening, then—the evening of Thursday, September 8th—the English were established at Barmoor, on the right side of the Till, their march having been executed within sight of Flodden Hill but safeguarded from interruption or attack by the river which ran between them and the Scottish troops. What Surrey's further intentions were must have remained doubtful. The original engagement on both sides to give battle on Friday, the 9th, would appear to have been forgotten or disregarded, since Surrey had invited the King to meet him on the previous day; and Holinshed's statement that James " thought it stood not with his honour to sit still and suffer himself to be forestalled forth of his own kingdom," would seem to point to a march into Scotland itself either contemplated by Surrey or feared by the King.

As to the action taken by James in consequence of the English change of tactics, uncertainty prevails; and theories and conjectures many and various have been hazarded on the subject. In the opinion of some historians the Scots continued to occupy their position fronting southward in spite of the fact that no enemy remained to face them in that direction. But it is clear that, whatever might be Surrey's ultimate intentions, his altered position rendered a corresponding move essential on the part of the Scots ; and disagreeing, on grounds of common sense, with the majority of writers, Colonel Elliot arrives at the conclusion that James quitted Flodden Hill on Thursday evening or Friday morning, to occupy the lower ground facing east in the direction of the enemy.

If this view is correct, the two armies, on the morning of the day when the battle was to be fought, were within sight of one another, with the river Till between, whilst it is asserted by one authority—Ridpath—that a battery of Scottish cannon had been erected east of Flodden Hill and bearing full upon the bridge of Ford.

On the morning of September 9th Surrey was again on the move. Whether or not he had ever meditated remaining where he was and so starving out the enemy, or had thought of marching upon Scotland, he now appeared to have determined to force an immediate action. With the main body of his troops he marched northward to Twizel, crossed the river Till by the bridge—the Scots having unaccountably permitted him to reach it undisturbed—and having gained the left bank of the river, turned his steps once more southward. His son, the admiral, who had preceded his father across the bridge, though taking a different route to the main body, moved in the same direction.

By this means Surrey was therefore north of the Scottish army and in a position to block the way should James, at last, have reconsidered his determination to give battle and attempted to retreat. When the two bodies of the English, converging towards the same point, met, it seems likely that it was at Branxton, a place not far from where the Scottish army was drawn up, that the junction was effected. It was first reached by Lord Thomas Howard, and hence he sent, as will be seen, to hasten his father's approach.

CHAPTER XIX

1513

The battle imminent—Signs and omens—Borthwick the
master-gunner—The camp fired—Obscurity as to the
battle itself—Stories and traditions—The defeat—
The King missing.

WHAT were the Scots doing whilst Surrey was
moving by his circuitous route towards the
field of battle ?

According to one chronicler[1] James had
hurriedly descended from the hill of Flodden
to place himself straightway on another hill,
presumably that of Branxton.   The reason
given for the move—namely, the King's apprehension that a foray into Scotland was intended
—does not explain his quitting Flodden to
establish himself at another spot only slightly
to the north of it, and it has already been shown
that the original camp had probably been
abandoned overnight.   If this was the case it
would have been the low ground then occupied

[1] Hall.

which was exchanged for the stronger position
afforded by Branxton Hill when it was made
clear that Surrey, instead of crossing the
Tweed, had gained the left bank of the Till
and was making his way southward. A battle
was plainly imminent, and it became of the
first importance to choose the ground on which
it would be fought.

On the whole, it is likely enough that James
would have welcomed the certainty that the
struggle was to take place. Apart from his
personal love of fighting, the only possible
alternative, now that Surrey barred the path
homeward, would have meant the prolonging
of a situation rendered daily more hazardous.

Yet the signs and omens noted in the camp
indicate an absence of that spirit of confidence
which is an earnest of success. Though these
warnings were regarded by some as mere acci-
dents—" casual haps "—it was observed that
they produced their impression on the King, in
" a certain religious fear and new terror." [1]

As he sat in council with his lords when the
order of battle was to be determined upon, a
hare started amongst the assembled nobles ;
and, in spite of the arrows and daggers dis-

[1] Holinshed.

charged at her with great noise and shouting, made good her escape. That night mice gnawed in sunder the buckle and leather of the King's helmet. Finally, at dawn " the cloth or veil of his inner tent (as is said) about the break of day appeared as though the dewy moisture thereof had been of a bloody colour."

Whether or not these premonitions of disaster did in truth cloud the King's mind, it was too late to draw back. Nor was he the man to attempt to escape the trial of strength he had invited. A story told by Pitscottie—and it may contain a measure of truth—shows him on the contrary eager for the fray. It is related that when the English were crossing the Till, Borthwick, the master-gunner, came into the presence of the King, and fell on his knees, desiring of the King's Grace that he might shoot his artillery at the English host . . . "promising that the bridge should be destroyed and the forces of the enemy thus separated, and one half left upon the other side of the river." And the story goes on to tell that James made answer, " like a man that had been reft of his wit, saying to him, ' I shall hang thee, quarter thee, and draw thee, if thou shoot one shot this day. I am determined that I will have them all before me on a plain field, and see what they can do all before me.' ''

That the passage refers to the crossing of the main body of the English troops at Twizel is clearly impossible. But Surrey might have left a contingent with orders to join him by a shorter and more hazardous route, and it may be at the bridges either of Etal or Ford that the master-gunner desired to direct his fire.

Before shifting their camp, on the approach of the English forces, from the lower ground to Branxton Hill, the Scots appear to have set fire, according to a common custom, to the huts they left behind, the smoke arising from the fire being so thick and dark as to conceal them for a time from the enemy. When it dispersed and the air became once more fair and clear, Thomas Howard was at hand and, becoming aware of the near neighbourhood of the enemy, he despatched a messenger in urgent haste to his father, sending the Agnus Dei he wore at his breast as a token that Surrey should advance to his support without delay.[1]

It was afternoon—some say as late as four o'clock—when the two armies met. The combat was after all to take place on the day

[1] Hall.

originally fixed, and not even to be post-
poned until the morrow, when both would
have had time to rest. Various causes may
have contributed to render the leaders on
either side anxious to try conclusions without
delay. Both armies were probably short of
food, more especially the Scots, in a foreign
and unfriendly country, and the provisions
they had carried with them exhausted. The
restlessness which finds further suspense un-
endurable may likewise have been felt, whilst
the fact that the 9th had been fixed as the
day of meeting, though disregarded meanwhile,
may have had its effect in determining the decision. At all events, the battle was to be
fought.

Of that battle a detailed account cannot be
given here. Nor will an exhaustive examination be made as to the degrees of credibility
attaching to the divers and often conflicting
accounts given of it by contemporary chroniclers
and later historians. Volumes on the subject
may be studied by the curious, and theories
have been elaborated both of what may be
imagined to have actually happened and of
what might have been the result had the plan
of action of the antagonists been other than it

was. Some of the accounts of the course of the fight, manifestly incompatible, must be false, and it is difficult to assign to each its true value.

Up to this point the movements of the opposed forces have been fairly ascertained. With regard to the fight that was to follow, "the real truth," admits Colonel Elliot, after a thorough investigation, carried out from the point of view both of the soldier and of the student, of all available documents—"the real truth is that all is conjecture, save the broad facts that, on the morning after the battle, the English army alone was on the field, the Scottish army—one division perhaps excepted—had gone; their dead lay thick upon the moor, their guns were abandoned, their King missing." [1]

Yet those hours had none the less a history, and from the pages of the chroniclers who profess to record it some idea may at least be gained of what was believed by contemporaries and by those who followed close upon contemporaries. Though liable to error and misled, it may be, at times by racial or national pre-

[1] It is curious, such being the case, to read the detailed accounts, given by various writers, of the course of the battle.

judice, authorities such as these, representing the traditions, if no more, belonging to that melancholy ninth of September cannot be wholly disregarded.

With respect to the order of battle, it would seem that the King, commanding in person the central body of the Scottish army, was confronted by Surrey, and that the old friendly antagonists here met, for the last time, in an almost hand-to-hand fight. Home and Huntley, on the left, headed the Scottish vanguard; and Lennox and Argyle led the right wing. The battle had soon begun—if it was to be decided before nightfall there was little time to lose—and at first it seemed uncertain to which side victory inclined. But not for long. To Home and Huntley the solitary gleam of real success on the Scottish side belonged. Face to face with the English troops under the admiral, Thomas Howard, his brother Edmund, and Sir Marmaduke Constable, the left wing of the Scots drove back the enemy. Edmund Howard in particular was thrice thrown to the ground, remaining at length alone, save for his standard-bearer and two servants; when John Heron, the bastard, the murderer of Ker, came, himself suffering from wounds, to his help.

" There was never nobleman's son so like to be lost as you be this day," he said. "For all my hurts I shall live and die with you."

Howard did in fact escape, killing Lord Home's brother David as he did so ; but the English under him were defeated.

Meantime, in the centre, the King was hard pressed. Of authentic particulars of his last fight there are none. The confusion of the day, the hurrying entanglements of the struggle on different parts of the field, is felt in the accounts of it ; even James's figure is lost, merged in the general mêlée. Yet it is plain that the rashness of his youth—the " young adventurousness "—had not even now been exchanged for the prudence and caution years might have been expected to bring, and that he flung himself into the fight like any common irresponsible soldier, regardless of the fact that the fate of his kingdom hung in great measure on his life—that he was the " rose noble " Scotland had staked, and that her destiny was linked with his. " O, what a noble and triumphant courage was this," exclaims Hall, " for a King to fight in a battle as a mean soldier. But howsoever it happen that God gave this stroke and he was no more regarded than a poor soldier, for all went one way."

And that way was the way of death.

Lord Home has been accused, truly or falsely, of a failure to go to the support of the King in his necessity.[1] Of his accusers Lindsay of Pitscottie is the mouthpiece, when he reports a dialogue alleged to have taken place between him and the Earl of Huntley after the success they had achieved. To Huntley's suggestion that Home should go to the rescue of the King in his extremity, Home is represented as replying by a flat refusal.

"He does well," he said, "that does for himself, for we have fought our vanguard and won the same, and therefore let the rest do their parts as well as we have done."

Huntley, more loyal, declared that he could not see his prince overcome by his enemies before his eyes and, calling his men together, would have hastened to James's help, "but or he came all was defeat, and very few alive."

Such is Lindsay's tale. Another chronicler[2]

[1] Colonel Elliot wholly acquits him of any misconduct, and considers the charge of treachery afterwards brought against him an absurdity.

[2] Polydore Vergil, tr. Gregory Smith, *The Days of James IV*.

corroborates it, saying that " although Alexander Home, the Lord Chamberlain who commanded a part of the army, saw his countrymen perishing, and hemmed in both in front and in the rear by the enemy, nevertheless he took no thought of sending succour, and did not move even a foot from the place where he was standing. When the rashness of the King became manifest, a stupor clouded the minds of all, just as some unwonted sleep will enchain the limbs. Each man, viewing his neighbour, stood motionless, and despaired, after the King had fallen, of being able to win the glorious victory which, by some strange chance, had fallen, as it were, from their hands."

Whatever else is doubtful, the defeat of the King's forces is certain. It is not known how long the battle lasted. All is confusion ; accounts vary, corroborate one another, conflict. James is said to have fallen not a lance's length from where Surrey in person was fighting ; again, it is stated that his body was found by Lord Dacre only on the following day ; then, that it was not found at all. No one had leisure even to ascertain the fate of the King. Everywhere men were fighting for their lives, falling, flying. Darkness was closing in upon the

19

struggle. It is vain to attempt to disentangle its several threads.

The sun set on that September evening at six o'clock, and night as it closed in was the best auxiliary the Scots could have. Had more hours of light remained, the disaster, great thou gh it was, would have been still greater. "If the day had been longer by three hours . . . or if the Englishmen had had victuals, so that they might have bidden still together, they had not only made the greatest distress of Scots by death and taking, that the like hath not been seen in one day, but also within a little while might have put the realm of Scotland in such a misery and trouble that for ever they should have been ware how to enter the realm of England." [1]

It is said that when darkness put an end to the combat neither party clearly knew who were the victors; and though this may be scarcely credible, the decisive nature of the fight may have been unsuspected by those who had taken part in it. It cannot be doubted that if Surrey had been aware of the completeness of his success, and the entire rout of the enemy, he would not have rested content with

[1] Hall.

the triumph he had achieved, when he might have taken advantage of it to press on into Scotland and have reached Edinburgh itself without danger of encountering effective resistance. Only when day broke, however, was it discovered that, if not all, the vast majority of the Scottish survivors were gone, that the field of battle was strewn with the flower of their army,[1] and lastly, and chief of all, that their King, like any common trooper, was "missing."

Thus ended the calamitous battle of Flodden Field.

> All the Scots that were scaped
> Were scattered far asunder.
> They removed over the moor
> Upon the next morning,
> And there stood like statues,
> And stir durst no further;
> For all the lords of their land
> Were left them behind !
> Beside Branxton in a brook
> Breathless they lie,
> Gaping against the moon
> Their ghosts went away ![2]

[1] It is computed that the slain included ten earls, eleven barons, the Archbishop of St. Andrews, with three other Church dignitaries, the Treasurer, and sixty-eight knights and gentlemen.

[2] "The Scottish Field," Lyme MSS. Quoted in *The Days of James IV.*, G. Gregory Smith.

CHAPTER XX

1513

THE King was missing. The "rose noble" of Scotland had been risked and lost. So much, as the sun rose on September 10th, was certain. Anything further concerning the fate of James Stewart remains matter of surmise; nor does the strange obscurity hanging over the history of his last battle lift to show how or where he met his death. It is likely, it is not likely— these are the only terms in which the matter can be discussed.

Ill news travels apace. On the very day after the battle the rumour, though unconfirmed, of an overwhelming disaster had spread in Edinburgh, and the proclamation issued by the city authorities gives proof alike of the consternation that reigned and of the stern and courageous spirit with which an unexampled national calamity was met :

"Forasmuch as there is a great rumour now lately risen within this town, touching our Sovereign Lord and his army, of which we understand there is come no verity as yet, wherefore we charge strictly and command, in our said Sovereign Lord, the King's name, and in that of the Presidents for the Provosts and Baillies within this burgh, that all manner of persons, townsmen within the same, have ready their arms of defence and weapons for war, and appear therewith before the said Presidents at the tolling of the common bell, for the keeping and defence of the town against them that would invade the same. And we also charge that all women, and especially vagabonds, that they pass to their labours, and be not seen upon the street clamouring and crying, under the pain of banishing of their persons without favour, and that the other women of better sort pass to the kirk and pray, when time requires, for our Sovereign Lord and his army, and the townsmen who are with the army ; and that they hold them at their private labours off the street within their houses, as becometh."

Thus James's capital prepared to meet whatever danger might threaten it. Meanwhile, where was he? By whose hands had he fallen? None could tell.

The authorised English version relates that a body found upon the field of battle "having divers deadly wounds and in especial one with an arrow and another with a bill," was recognised as that of the dead King, Lord Dacre claiming the distinction of having made the discovery. "They love me worst of any Englishman living," he wrote to the English Council in reference to the Scots, "by reason that I found the body of the King of Scots, slain in the field. . . ." The corpse was carried to Berwick and was there displayed to James's Chancellor, Sir William Scot, and Sir John Forman, his Serjeant porter—the only prisoners of note taken alive—who identified it as that of their master and made great lamentation. It was then embalmed and conveyed first to Newcastle, whence it was brought to Richmond to the Carthusian monastery at Bethlehem. Though the King had died excommunicate, Leo X gave Henry VIII permission to bury him in consecrated ground at St. Paul's Cathedral, but there is no evidence to show

that this was done, and Stow asserts that, on
the dissolution of the religious houses in Edward
VI's reign, the body was still lying, lapped in
lead, in a waste room, amongst old timber and
rubble."[1]

The account is detailed and complete. Yet
by many, both at the time and since, it has
been a matter of grave doubt whether the body
thus treated was indeed that of James. Ten
men besides the King wore the royal armour
on the fatal day with the object of misleading
the enemy, two of whom in particular, members
of his guard, resembled him in make and build ;
and it was thought that a confusion might have
thus arisen, the rather because the body carried
south wore no iron belt. "True it is," says
Lindsay, "they got not the King, because
they have never the token of his iron belt to
show to no Scottish man."

Tales were likewise current, and were widely
credited, to the effect that the King was
alive, and that there were those who had seen

---

[1] Stow adds an improbable story, telling how workmen,
"for their foolish pleasure," hewed off the head, and Young,
Queen Elizabeth's master glazier, kept the ghastly trophy
for a time in his house in Wood Street, causing it at last
to be buried by the sexton of St. Michael's Church amongst
other bones.

him after the battle. A page of his own affirmed that he had watched him on the following day ride across the Tweed ; he had been also seen at Kelso ; others, clinging to the belief that the man they loved so well had not perished, asserted that he had taken his way to Jerusalem in performance of his vow. " The common people," says Drummond, " believed he was living, and had passed over the seas, and according to his promise visited the Holy Sepulchre in Palestine. There for his other offences and the bearing of arms against his father, in prayers and penances he spent the remainder of his tedious days. That he would return again when he found opportunity and the necessity of Europe required it."

With regard to this legend of his survival it is a strange fact that, from a document amongst the State papers, it appears that Queen Margaret, when desirous of obtaining a divorce from her second husband, the young Earl of Angus, married by her within a twelvemonth of the battle of Flodden, declared that James had lived for three years after it and that her marriage was therefore invalid and void.[1]

The disappearance of the King has been

---

[1] *Battle of Flodden*, Elliot.

explained in another and more sinister fashion.
A dark rumour connected Lord Home with
it, on the hypothesis—or so it would seem—
that he feared chastisement, should James live
to give it, for his failure to afford him support
on the field of battle. It was alleged that one
of Home's servants afterwards hinted that
he had helped to teach a Scottish King that
he was mortal ;[1] and ten years later, a man
under sentence of death is reported to have
offered, on condition of receiving a free pardon,
to show the regent, Albany, where the King
was buried, his iron belt beside him. "But
this man got no audience by them that was
about him, and the Duke of Albany desired
not that such things should be known."[2]

The legends that gather round the life and
death of a popular hero die hard. In comparatively recent times a curious proof was
given of the vitality of the tradition that
associates Lord Home with the King's end. "I
recollect," says Sir Walter Scott in the *Tales
of a Grandfather*, "about forty years ago, that
there was a report that in clearing the draw-
well of that ruinous fortress [Home Castle] the
workmen found a skeleton wrapt in a bull's

---

[1] Drummond.   [2] Lindsay of Pitscottie.

hide, and having a belt of iron round the waist. There was, however, no truth in this rumour." [1]

If, as Colonel Elliot, after careful examination, believes, there had been nothing in Home's conduct to call for blame from his master, all motive for the crime disappears. " Home was a friend of the King's ; by his death he had everything to lose, nothing to gain ; to murder him would have been contrary not only to his feelings, but to his interests." If, it may be added, he had indeed secret reasons for desiring James's death, there were surely simpler and safer ways of compassing it, in the darkness and confusion of the battlefield, than by conveying him to a distance, there to be destroyed.

Howsoever it may have come about, it is a singular and tragic conclusion to James's life-story that the man who, ever since his boyhood, had stood in the full light, before the eyes of the world, a brilliant and noteworthy figure, should lie in a nameless and unhonoured grave ; that he should have met his end no man can surely say how or in what fashion ; and that it was by a path that none can trace with certainty that he reached " the house of Death,

---

[1] This story is also told in Grose's *Antiquities of Scotland*, vol. ii. p. 232 *note*.

whose doors be open at all hours and to all persons."

Alive, he had been well loved. Dead, he was not forgotten, for "such a desire remained of him in the hearts of his people after his loss that the like was not of any King before him."

APPENDIX

OF the many accounts of the battle of Flodden in prose and verse the well-known description of it given by Sir Walter Scott in *Marmion,* is, of course, the most famous. Amongst other poems on the subject Sir David Lyndsay's *Lament* serves as a description of James by a man who knew him, and may therefore be fitly given here. It was written about the year 1530 :

> Alas ! where be that right redoubted roy,
>> That potent prince, gentil King James the Fierd !
> I pray to Christ his soul for to convoy :
>> A greater noble rang not into the eird.
>> O Atropus ! warye we may thy weird ;
> For he was mirror of humility,
> Lodestar and lamp of liberality.
>
> During his time, so justice did prevail,
>> The savage isles trembled for terrour ;
> Esdale, Evisdale, Liddisdale, and Annandale
>> Durst not rebel, doubting his dyntis dour ;
>> And of his lords had such perfect favour ;
> So for to show that he a-feared no fone,
> Out through his realm he would ride him alone.

And of his court through Europe sprang the fame,
   Of lusty lords and lovesome ladies ying,
Triumphant tourneys, jousting, and knightly game,
   With all pastime, according for a King :
   He was the glore of princely governing,
Who, through the ardent love he had to France,
Against England did move his ordinance.

Of Flodden Field the ruin to revolve,
   Or that most dolent day for to deplore,
I nill, for dread for dolour you dissolve,
   Show how that prince in his triumphant glore,
   Destroyed was—what needeth process more ?
Not by the virtue of English ordinance
But by his own wilful misgovernance.

Alas ! that day had he been counselable,
   He had obtained laud, glore, and victory ;
Whose piteous process be so lamentable,
   I nill at length it put in memory.
   I never read in tragedy or story
At one journey so many nobles slain
For the defence and love of their sovereign.

INDEX

A

Ainslow, his news letter, 219

Albany, Alexander Stewart, Duke of, brother to James III, 3, 4, 12, 13 ; in confinement, 15 ; his escape, 16, 17 ; joins the English, 22, 24 ; flight to France and death there, 34

Alexander VI, Pope, 145

Angoulême, Duc d', 196

Angus, Earl of, 20, 25 seq., 169, 185, 272-4

Angus, Earl of, Queen Margaret's second husband, 290

Anne of Brittany, Queen of France, her love-letter to James IV, 241, 242 ; Margaret jealous of, 255

Anne, daughter of Duke of Suffolk, James IV betrothed to, 35, 79

Argyle, Earl of, 286

Arran, Earl of, imprisoned by Henry VII, 190 seq. ; in command of the fleet, 240, 243

Arthur, Prince, of England, 145, 208, 216, 222

Arthur, Prince, of Scotland, birth and death of, 205

Aubigny, Bernard d', French envoy, 195-7

Ayala, Don Pedro de, at James's court, 123 ; his description of James, 124-7 ; negotiates peace with England, 128, 140, 141, 142, 165

Aytoun, truce of, 129

B

Bamborough, burnt by Earl of Angus, 20

Barton, the family of sailors, 56

Barton, Andrew, 199, 200, 211, 212, 246, 269

Barton, John, 199

Barton, Robert, 176, 199, 200, 201, 202, 218

Blackness, burnt, 21

Borthwick, murderer of James III, 51, 52

Borthwick, James IV's master gunner, 282, 283

Bothwell. *See* Ramsay, Hepburn, and Kennedy

Boyd clan, the, 5

Boyd, Marion, James IV's mistress, 186

Buchan, Earl of, 62, 101, 107

Bulmer, Sir W., 266

Burgundy, Duchess of, 84, 87, 89, 105, 106

C

Cambrai, League of, 207

Cecilia, Princess, betrothed to James IV, 10 ; and to Earl of Albany, 23 ; her betrothal to James cancelled, 34, 79

Charles, King of Castile, 196

Charles VIII, King of France, 84, 102, 114

Christian, King of Denmark, 2

Christina, Queen of Denmark, 175, 176

Cochrane, James III's favourite, 8, 13 ; made Earl of Mar, 17, 18 ; killed at Lauder, 24-9

Coldingham Priory, 38

Concressault, French envoy, 102, 104

Constable, Sir Marmaduke, 266 ; at Flodden, 286

in Scotland, 87; interview with James, 91; James adopts his cause, 92; Ramsay's account of, 100 seq.; expedition to England, 109; its failure, ibid., 111; an inconvenient guest, 113–15; dismissed by James, 116, 117

West, Dr., envoy to Scotland, his reports, 221–32

Wolsey, Thomas, envoy to Scotland, 191 seq.

Wood, Sir Andrew, 54–6; exploits at sea, 69, 70, 176, 201, 243

Y

York, Cardinal of, 224

York, Richard, Duke of. *See* Warbeck.

Young, John, Somerset Herald, his account of Margaret's journey and arrival in Scotland, 151 seq.

Printed by Hazell, Watson & Viney, Ld., London and Aylesbury.